ANTI-SEMITISM REVISITED

DELPHINE HORVILLEUR

ANTI-SEMITISM REVISITED

How the Rabbis Made Sense Of Hatred

Translated from the French by
David Bellos

MACLEHOSE PRESS
QUERCUS · LONDON

First published as *Réflexions sur la question antisémite*
by Editions Grasset, Paris, in 2019
First published in Great Britain in 2021 by MacLehose Press
This paperback edition published in 2022 by

MacLehose Press
An imprint of Quercus Publishing Ltd
Carmelite House
50 Victoria Embankment
London EC4Y 0DZ

An Hachette UK company

The authorised representative in the EEA is Hachette Ireland, 8 Castlecourt
Centre, Dublin 15, D15 XTP3, Ireland (email: info@hbgi.ie)

A CIP catalogue record for this book is available from the British Library.

ISBN (MMP) 978 1 52940 476 0
ISBN (Ebook) 978 0 85705 902 4

2 4 6 8 10 9 7 5 3

Designed and typeset in Haarlemmer by Libanus Press Ltd
Printed and bound in Great Britain by Clays Ltd, Elcograf S.p.A.

In memory of Simone and Marceline, "daughters of Birkenau", who taught us how to live

In memory of Sarah and Isidore, my grandparents, who both survived and lived less than they should

What have I in common with Jews? I have hardly anything in common with myself, and should stand very quietly in a corner, content that I can breathe.

Franz Kafka, *Diaries*

CONTENTS

Translator's note

Quotations from Tanakh, Talmud, Torah, Mishnah and Midrash are given in the form provided by Sefaria.org. I am grateful to the many volunteer scholars who have made this precious resource available online.

Translations of quotations from other sources are my own if not otherwise attributed.

Introduction

"Jews are just too much . . ."[1]

There's no denying that we've never been liked very much. But why is it that Jews aren't liked? For a start, we're not Gentiles, and if you're speaking in French, that also says we're not nice. It's a hoary old joke, but it is true that anti-Semites have always objected to Jews not being part of the family, which is what *gentilis* means in Latin (strictly speaking, members of a family bearing the same name). As Jews aren't Gentiles, they are always outside the group, and therefore a threat to it. "They're not like us" is a common refrain. The supposed differentness of Jews can become a mental obsession, or else a cause of disgust. But Jew-hating is not just another variety of the hatred of the foreign. It has features that make it unique.

The basic distinction between anti-Semitism and other kinds of racism is this. Racist ideology generally articulates hatred of the other for what the other does not have—the

1 Louis-Ferdinand Céline, *Bagatelles pour un massacre* (Paris: Denoël, 1938), p. 319.

same skin colour, for instance, or the same customs, cultural practices or language. The racist sees what is "not like me" in the other as being "less than me", which makes the other instantly imperfect or inferior. Others are *barbarians* in the Greek sense of the word—people who when they speak make primitive, comical stammering sounds: *ba-ba-bar* . . .

Jews, by contrast, are often hated not for what they DO NOT have, but for what they HAVE. Jews aren't attacked for having less than non-Jews, but for having probably usurped things that belong by right to non-Jews. Jews are accused of grabbing and holding on to power, money, privileges and distinctions that others can't get their hands on.

So Jews are therefore imagined as owners of a "something extra" that non-Jews can't acquire. Throughout history, Jews have often been described as troublemakers who subvert, capture or poison common property, making it all but impossible to divide it into fair shares for everyone else. Jews may speak the same language and live in the same neighbourhoods as non-Jews, but in the eyes of their enemies they seem to do these things a little more than others do, with greater arrogance or greater ease. No change of attitude or speech among Jews could assuage such resentment and envy. In all circumstances, Jews are "excessive", literally: there's something about them that is "too much", more than is needed, or at any rate "more than I've got".

The first thing they have more of is length of existence. Jews are exasperatingly long-lasting. They just won't disappear! Such historical endurance is an intolerable impertinence. Why can't Jews die out like everyone else and sink into oblivion, like other civilisations have managed to do? Their persistence is really irritating. Even their suffering knows no end! After each disaster they rise up again and oblige their persecutors to resent them even more for having suffered to a higher degree. Even in that domain, Jews have something "extra" that deprives others: the greater visibility of their suffering makes people wonder why their own histories aren't just as worthy of lamentation. That's why it's so hard to forgive Jews the harm done to them . . . The intensity of Jews' suffering also seems over the top. Paradoxically, their long standing as victims and as targets of discrimination, which ought to function logically as a "less than me", has come to serve as a "more than me", an advantage that others envy.

Jew-hatred also has another special feature: it allows Jews to be accused of polar opposites at the same time. Over the centuries, anti-Semites have never had a problem reproaching Jews simultaneously for some flaw and for its exact opposite: they have too much money, obviously, but they're also parasites leeching on the nation's resources.

Jews have been denounced as excessively socialist, and as excessively bourgeois too. They've been seen as threats to the "system" and also as pillars of it. They've been blamed for not believing in Jesus and for having invented him; for being cloaked in mystery and being a bit too visible; for blending in so well as to be no longer clearly identifiable, and for marrying only their own kind and keeping to themselves. In a word, Jews are always a bit too much the same and a bit too different. Jews dare to assimilate over here, and to claim sovereign status over there; they have the effrontery to stay, and the sheer cheek to go.

Anti-Semites claim they can identify Jews one hundred per cent, because Jews' gestures, like their noses, their hair, their tones of voice and their gaits, are just unmistakable. In which case, why do anti-Semites spend so much effort hunting them down as if they were tracking some invisible spoor in the dark? Until 2012, when legal action was taken to stop this, you could type the name of any celebrity in Google's search bar and be offered links to the term "Jewish" attached to the name. The French President+ Jewish . . . George Clooney+Jewish . . . How about Father Christmas?

The appearance of the word "Jewish" in the search bar was the effect of an algorithm drawing on the highest-ranking frequencies of other Web users' searches. It there-fore displayed the frantic nature of these kinds of enquiries.

Jew-hunting is an obsessive quest to find dormant Jewishness in every one of the masters of the world and to make it manifest by navigating on the Web. Watch out for Jews! There may be one right beside you—in your office, on your street, among your books. They keep it under wraps. They'll never tell you the truth.

CHAPTER ONE

Anti-Semitism Is a Family Quarrel

Anti-Jewish fury is an ancient evil that is always different and yet always the same, despite the widely varying contexts in which it rears its ugly head.

The roots of this curse have been studied by scholars in many disciplines: historians, sociologists, theologians and psychologists have tried to understand the political, economic, social and religious reasons for the emergence and repeated resurgence of anti-Semitism. Far fewer have used Jewish literature to see how Jews themselves have interpreted the phenomenon.

It is not the job of the victims of violence or discrimination to explain the causes of the hatred that afflicts them or to analyse their persecutors' motives. I surely don't need to stress this point. Anti-Semitism is not a "Jewish problem" but always, primarily, a problem for anti-Semites and for the people who allow them to exist and give them support. Anyway, why should scholars of Jewish Scripture have a special key for understanding this hatred?

Jewish lore won't answer every question, but it can

unlock some doors. Judaism's own ways of dealing with anti-Jewish hatred show us, uniquely, how a whole people passed on its subjective experience to warn later generations and alert them to the re-emergence of the evil and to the possibility of recovering from it. Rabbinical interpretation shows us how to understand what happened to Jews in specific historical contexts—how to receive the story of past suffering; but it gives us even more insight into the rabbis' thinking about the origin of the phenomenon, and about how an afflicted community can cope with it. Rabbinical literature aims to give Jews the chance of reasserting their historical agency when confronting what might recur. It also provides unique insight into oppressors' minds as they were understood by the vulnerable party seeking its own protection. It does not lock the victim into its own pain, nor does it—perhaps surprisingly—confine perpetrators to their own hatred. The refusal of such fatalism is what it behoves us to explore for our own times.

In a nutshell: how do the sages and the texts of Jewish tradition interpret the chronic affliction of the anger expressed against them? Is there a specifically Jewish understanding of anti-Semitism?

Jewish non-identity

Where are the origins of anti-Semitic hatred to be found in Jewish Scripture? The Torah, called the Old Testament by Christians, says nothing about anti-Jewish hatred. It says nothing for the good reason that the Torah is not about Jews. The people whose story it tells are called Hebrews, or children of Israel, at the time of the events. At a much later date in history, Jews claimed descent from these two identities.

Let us take a closer look at the terms of Jewish proto-identity.

The first of the Hebrews was called Abraham, and he was born in the city of Ur, in the land of the Chaldees. He was not born a Hebrew in an ancestral Hebrew land, but acquired that new identity by leaving home ... at the behest of a divinity encouraging him to leave his father's land and his birthplace behind him: "The Lord said to Abram, 'Go forth from your native land and from your father's house to the land that I will show you'" (Genesis 12:1). So off he goes to cross a river that will lead him towards a promised land whose name, he later learns, is Canaan.

In Hebrew, the word for "Hebrew", *Ivri*, means "he who crosses", or "passer-by". Because he left the land of his birth and origin, Abraham acquired a label that names his action, which is the word for "crossing over".

The Hebrew identity that arises with Abraham is therefore an identity of being torn from a native land. It is not tied to a territorial origin, a place of beginning. That is rather special in the ancient world. Egyptians come from Egypt, Greeks from Greece, Romans from Rome, but the name of the Hebrews doesn't say where they come from at all: only that they come from *somewhere else*. That is at the root of a subtle ambiguity in Hebrew identity, which became a Jewish one later on.

A Hebrew is not a person who comes from somewhere, but someone who has set out to travel away from his birthplace. Hebrew identity therefore asserts through its very name that its origin lies only in having left it: it's an identity based on non-identity with the place it comes from. "Against the myth of Ulysses returning to Ithaca, we can set the story of Abraham leaving his homeland for an unknown destination and even forbidding his servant ever to take his son back to the point of departure," wrote the philosopher Emmanuel Levinas.[2] "The Promised Land is the desire for a land not of our birth . . . and to which we will never betake ourselves."[3]

So in the beginning is the break. This is a central idea in

2 E. Levinas, "La trace de l'autre", *Tijdschrift voor Filosofie* 25:3 (1963), pp. 605–23.
3 E. Levinas, *Totality and Infinity* [1961], trans. Alphonso Lingis (Pittsburgh: Duquesne University Press, 1969), p. 36.

the impossible definition of what Jewishness is. It is brilliantly illustrated in the way Jacques Derrida described his own Jewishness: it is, he says, "the other name for the impossibility of being myself".

Long after Abraham came down from Mesopotamia, the Hebrews, at a key moment in their history, repeated the pattern of separation collectively, when they came down from Egypt.

Chaldea may have been the land of Abraham's fathers, but in the Torah the Nile Delta is the real womb of the people. That is the place where Jacob's seed settled and multiplied until the womb of Egypt opened. The plagues of Egypt, likened to birthing pains by some commentators, set off the labour and the delivery. The seas open, the people leave a land still called *Um-el-Dunya*, or "mother of the world", in Arabic today, under orders never to return. So off they go towards the Promised Land.

The people was thus born in Egypt and once again the founding event of its collective identity is a departure, a rupture that gives it existence in non-identity to the place where it was born.

A name that limps

The other biblical designation of this people, "people of Israel", tells a strangely similar story. The name "Israel" first crops up in another episode where identity is broken. Genesis tells the story of one of Abraham's grandsons, Jacob, who stops for the night on the bank of a river he has to cross. In the dark Jacob has to struggle with a mysterious messenger, who may be an angel or a man, and who wounds him in the hip but offers him a strange blessing at dawn: "Your name shall no longer be Jacob, but Israel, for you have striven with beings divine and human, and have prevailed" (Genesis 32:29).

This name won in combat and handed on to Jacob's descendants is therefore not an origin name, but an identity gained from a struggle at the cost of a dislocated hip, which guarantees that he will limp ever after.

Jacob-Israel has been torn from his identity of birth and knows he will never stand up straight again. To stay upright is a balancing act that requires constant movement. Henceforth he is here and then there, going back and forth between two states and keeping upright only by swinging first this way and then that. In permanent movement, he has to *become* in order to *be*, and can only ever *be* through *becoming*.

The Torah thus tells the story of the Hebrews and the

sons of Israel as a journey away from places of birth towards a Promised Land they never reach at any point in the tale: they are still on their way when we get to the last line of the text.

But the Torah says absolutely nothing about Jews. At least, not in the sense in which we use the term today to designate the religious affiliation of a group. When it appears in the Torah, *yehudi*, the Hebrew word for "Jew", applies either to a tribe or to a place (the tribe of Judah, or the place we now call Judea), but never to the religious identity of a group.

Jews arise in Scripture at a much later stage, in a different book, in a different era and in a different land. To get acquainted with them we have to open the door of a famous Bible story that bears a woman's name: Esther.

Find the lady

It happened in the realm of King Assuerus, which spread across a large part of ancient Persia. One day, on the advice of his counsellors, the king repudiated his wife Vashti and set about finding another, more submissive queen. The greatest beauty pageant in biblical history took place, and it was won by a girl called Esther, about whom the king knew very little. That is the meaning of the name in Hebrew:

Esther is "the hidden one", "the mysterious one". The king is unaware that she belongs to the children of Israel, who had been dispersed and sent into exile after the destruction of the first Temple. Nor does he know that she is the niece (or the wife, according to less politically correct rabbinical legends) of someone called Mordecai, "son of Yair son of Shimei son of Kish, a Benjaminite" (Esther 2:5).

Mordecai's genealogy makes him a descendant of the Hebrew tribe of Benjamin. But though Mordecai is a Benjaminite (and therefore does not belong to the tribe of Judah), he is always referred to in the Scripture as a *yehudi*. This is the first time in biblical literature that a person is given this label not as identification of geographical origin or as a sign of belonging to a province or a tribe, but as a name of a different kind. All of a sudden, the word refers to a collective identity, to a people, to membership of a group. Mordecai is therefore the first Jew in the history of Scripture.

Jewish identity as we would understand it today, as the name of a religious community or of a people dispersed, arose at some point in the Persian exile. Judaism, according to the Bible, is a product of exile, the condition of people dispossessed of their land of origin.

Esther arrives at the court of King Assuerus as a new queen cloaked in mystery. But scarcely has a Jew entered the palace in the guise of a woman than another equally essential character steps onto the stage: her enemy.

The bad guy in the book of Esther is Haman son of Agag. He is promoted to the rank of special adviser to the court of King Assuerus. On his heels comes hatred. For a strange reason that has been the object of endless speculation, Haman can't stand Mordecai. Is it jealousy? Old scores to be settled? Whatever the cause, Haman so detests Mordecai as to foment the extermination of all his people. He urges his sovereign Assuerus to authorise genocide and asks to be entrusted with implementing it.

At the start of the book of Esther, heinous Haman is granted a special audience with his king, where he says: "There is a certain people, scattered and dispersed among the other peoples in all the provinces of your realm, whose laws are different from those of any other people and who do not obey the king's laws; and it is not in Your Majesty's interest to tolerate them" (Esther 3:8). (More literally: "for the king it is not equal for them to stay".)

In a single verse Haman gives us a perfect summary and a timeless illustration of what the Jews have been accused of throughout history: they are a people seen as dispersed and separate, involved with others but refusing to be like them, undetectable but also unassimilable. Their particularity is felt to be a threat to the integrity of the nation or of political power and puts in jeopardy the rigorous equality between the different elements that make up an undivided nation. There therefore hovers over the Jewish people a suspicion of non-allegiance that ultimately justifies expulsion or physical elimination.

At the very point where Jews arise in Scripture—in the same breath, so to speak—an enemy arises, like a scary doppelgänger in some literary text.

Amalek

Where does the enemy of the Jews in the book of Esther come from? What is the source of his hatred? Exegetes explain that the story doesn't begin there, but in another story and, like detectives, they explore the genealogical trees of the first Jew and his legendary foe. So let us follow them up the track of the biblical generations of anti-Semitic hatred.

Mordecai is a descendant of Kish, that is to say, of Saul, the first king of Israel (1 Samuel 9:1–2 tells us that Saul was the son of Kish).

Haman is said to be a descendant of Agag (Esther 3:1), who was king of the Amalecites and the sworn enemy of Saul at the time of the latter's reign. The confrontation of Mordecai and Haman is thus a continuation of a conflict begun by their ancestors. They were still fighting the war that set Agag against Saul long before.

The genealogical trail does not stop there, however.

Agag was the head of the Amalecites, and therefore a descendant of another biblical character called Amalek. That adds another twist to the tangled story.

Much earlier on in the biblical narrative, Amalek undertook a war against the Hebrews. Deuteronomy, which is addressed to the people of Israel, puts it like this:

> Remember what Amalek did to you on your journey, after you left Egypt—how, undeterred by fear of God, he surprised you on the march, when you were famished and weary, and cut down all the stragglers in your rear. Therefore, when the LORD your God grants you safety from all your enemies around you, in the land that the LORD your God is giving you as a hereditary portion, you shall blot out the memory of Amalek from under heaven. Do not forget!
> [Deuteronomy 25:17–19]

What this means is that Amalek had attacked the Hebrews when they were in the desert just after their departure from Egypt, and had targeted the most vulnerable among them. He had tried to exterminate a people that had only just managed to free itself from slavery and was not ready for combat.

The memory of this particular onslaught passed down the generations through the admonition given by the

Scripture: *remember to suppress the memory of Amalek*. What a strange command! How can you remember not to remember? You can hardly expect an amnesiac to have an unforgettable experience. We shall return to this later on.

All the same, from this point on, the name of Amalek is associated with anti-Jewish hatred throughout history. Amalek becomes the tag-name that exegetes give to the Jews' worst enemies—Crusaders, Inquisitors, the bloodthirsty perpetrators of pogroms in Europe, down to the Nazis . . . all were at some point identified by rabbis as contemporary reincarnations of Amalek, as descendants of that fearsome biblical figure.

Accordingly, there arises in every epoch a descendant of Amalek, the archetype of the assassin consumed by hatred of Jews and intent on exterminating them. This archetypal reading of anti-Semitism presents the undying threat as a fate, as a repetition of ancient history, as the transmigration of hate.

That's why the tag "Amalek" is dropped into Scripture in direct connection with the ascendance of Haman, to be reactivated in the story of Persia. Haman being thus made the inheritor of an ancestral hatred, the book of Esther restages a conflict that has its roots elsewhere. Haman's anger came from Agag's and Agag's from Amalek's. But what caused Amalek's fury in the first place? The rabbis had to look elsewhere to find the next piece of the puzzle.

A bad start for anti-Semites

Biblical scholars have to go a little further up the family tree to find out who gave birth to Amalek. The answer can be found in Genesis, in the verse that gives the descent of Esau, Jacob's twin brother. Esau was the father of Eliphaz, who took a concubine, Timna, and "she bore Amalek to Eliphaz" (Genesis 36:12). That makes Amalek the grandson of Esau and the son of Eliphaz and his concubine Timna. Readers familiar with Scripture may have noticed that there is something unusual about this verse: it gives us both the name of the mother, Timna, and her status, concubine. Most of the time women are not included in biblical gene-alogies, save in a few cases where the woman mentioned is a legitimate spouse. Concubines are almost always kept in the background in these patriarchal stories. Timna stands out simply for being present—not only in Genesis, but also at the heart of another book, Chronicles, which recapitulates the major lines of descent from Genesis.

Here, we're in for a surprise. In Chronicles, the rela-tionship between Amalek and Timna is different. In the recitation of the descendants of Eliphaz, we read: "The sons of Eliphaz: Teman, Omar, Zephi, Gatam, Kenaz, Timna, and Amalek" (1 Chronicles 1:36).

In Genesis, Timna is Amalek's mother, whereas in Chronicles she is his sister. In rabbinical commentary, there is no question about it: Timna is one and the other. Eliphaz took his daughter as his concubine, and Amalek is a child of incest.

A rabbinical commentary adds that Timna was the child of an adulterous relationship between Eliphaz and the wife of a prince from the region of Seir: "He had sexual relations with Seir's wife first and made her pregnant and begot Timna. Later he married Timna, as though she were Seir's daughter, when in fact she was his own" (Midrash Tanchuma, Vayeshev 1). Adultery thus compounds incest, and makes Amalek's descent doubly transgressive.

Anti-Semitic mythologies

Taking this transgressive genealogy as a starting point, the commentaries written in the first centuries of the Common Era conclude that "this flawed line of descent remains unwholesome to this day" (Midrash Tanchuma). It's as if this act of incest, the moral and sexual misdemeanour in the line of Esau that gave birth to Amalek, would haunt the family down the ages and stain all its descendants with a moral flaw. For the rabbis who wrote Midrash, this is of course an allegorical reading: anti-Semitism is not in their minds a heritable disease in the sense we might use that term nowadays. But they do suggest we should investigate the notion of "inheritance" in the transmission of hatred. In their reading, something like a foundational transgression was passed down family lines; members of the line can never free themselves of it unless they confront it head-on.

Historically repetitious outbursts of hatred embodied in an Amalek who can reincarnate himself in each generation are thus analysed in the Midrash by means of a metaphor of a multigenerational stain. The rabbis saw the origin of such violence through the lens of the violation of the ultimate taboo against incest. They raise the question as to whether the hatred is not the unconscious inheritance of a genealogical flaw that descendants cannot eradicate. Seen from this admittedly simplistic point of view, anti-Semitism would be just a story of defectives bearing the stigma of sexual transgression that, like a psychosis, never stops re-enacting its own hatred against Jews.

But why against the Jews? Perhaps because, for their haters, Jews are often seen as the incarnation of the Law, the source of taboo and superior authority. On this view, Jews, by giving the Law to the world, come to represent it, and become living reminders of ancient crimes in family history.

If Amalek's violence derives from a defect in his family tree, then the symbolic bearers of the Law, that is to say, Jews, are constant reminders of the original flaw. They make it impossible to forget or erase it.

Unless . . .

Rabbinical writers, seemingly aware that no single account could explain everything, also pursue other disturbing possibilities. What if there was more to Timna's story? What if Amalek was someone else? In the Babylonian Talmud, we find just such questions asked about the identity of the mysterious concubine.

Timna and the repression of the origin

So who was Timna, this biological origin of the figure of evil? Was she Amalek's sister, or his mother? Did her own father abuse her, as legends claim? The Babylonian Talmud has a different suggestion.

In this alternative version, Timna was a young princess from the region of Seir and a prominent person in the locality. One day she felt drawn to Abraham, Isaac and Jacob, the tutelary figures of the Hebrews, and introduced herself to them with the intention of joining their spiritual community (that is to say, aiming to convert). However, the illustrious rabbinical tribunal composed of the three patriarchs turned her down, reckoning she had ulterior motives. Made spiteful by rejection, Timna turned to Eliphaz son of Esau and became his concubine. That's how she came to give birth to Amalek, whose subsequent career we know.

The Talmudic rabbis give a bold but anachronistic reading of Timna's story. Obviously, conversion to Judaism didn't exist in biblical times. Rabbinical tribunals also came into existence only centuries later, at the time the Talmud was being composed. Notwithstanding, the Babylonian rabbis saw Timna acting like one of the postulants they might have turned down themselves—except that she was rejected by the most glorious and prestigious tribunal that ever existed. For want of being allowed to join the Hebrews and the sons of Jacob, Timna allied herself with the seed of Esau, giving birth to Amalek, the child of spite, disappointment and exclusion, who presumably carried in himself his mother's pain.

Timna sought to convert. She came before Abraham, Isaac and Jacob, and they did not accept her. She went and became a concubine of Eliphaz, son of Esau, and said, referring to herself: It is preferable that she will be a maidservant for this nation, and she will not be a noblewoman for another nation. Ultimately, Amalek, son of Eliphaz, emerged from her, and that tribe afflicted the Jewish people. What is the reason that the Jewish people were punished by suffering at the hand of Amalek? It is due to the fact that they should not have rejected her when she sought to convert. [Babylonian Talmud, Sanhedrin 99b]

In this passage, the rabbis pursue a disturbing argument and imagine a different source for hatred of Jews: the spite and disappointment of a stranger not accepted and not welcomed into the family. In their eyes, Amalek was, so to speak, burdened with his mother's disappointment, with a frustrated, unrealised dream liable to turn into resentment. So the rabbis then wonder: what part of that is our own fault? How much suffering would have been avoided if we had accepted Timna and allowed her to join the family? Could we have prevented the birth of Amalek?

This path of reasoning is disturbing because it seems to lay part of the responsibility and the blame for anti-Semitism on Jews. It seems to imply that every subsequent generation of victims would be paying for their ancestors' intransigence, their inability to open wider the doors of the house of Israel. That's something that's hard to hear: anti-Semitism as the price to be paid by Jews for not accepting converts.

Unless we hear the story with different ears and take an alternative path along the same road. In this reading, the hatred nurtured by anti-Semites is not simply the result of a skeleton in the family cupboard or of inherited depravity, as the Midrash Tanchuma would have us believe. It becomes a tale of jealousy, desire and repression, of a frustrated aspiration to belong to a family that is not set on expansion or on imposing its own truth on the world. Jew-hatred is therefore the anger of an outsider against a clan that is the most clannish of all. "Why am I not allowed to join you?" Timna may have mumbled. The silencing of her words coupled with an inability to get over rejection and humiliation make the perfect mash for brewing hatred.

So that is how AMALEK was born: in Hebrew, his name literally means "he who has no people". He is the son of TIMNA, whose name means "rejected, held back". As is often the case with biblical characters, the names speak the fate.

What if anti-Semitism across the ages derived from a lack of belonging, from the need to be accepted, loved or recognised by another? The hater would aspire to be free of the feeling of exclusion and would wonder: how can Jews stay "among themselves" when I cannot be among them?

It must have taken some courage for the rabbis to go so far as to question their own role and to undertake an exercise in serious self-criticism by asking what their own unwillingness to make converts entailed. Their conclusion was: we should not have rejected Timna.

To what extent have the so often misunderstood notion of "chosen-ness" and the refusal to make converts fed the hatred of Jews? How can the transmission of fury from one generation to the next be halted?

From Haman to Amalek, from Amalek to Timna . . . We've found some clues. We're getting somewhere.

Everything suggests that in the eyes of the rabbis the figure of the anti-Semite, under its different disguises, always claimed to inherit pain from the past, or, to be more precise, it is as if anti-Semites could never extricate themselves from a past that weighs down on them, from an inherited suffering for which someone else has to pay. Jews are for them the reminders of what they should or could have been, and so hatred is handed on as an inability to recover from the challenge and to see themselves as anything other than children of a mistake, the heirs of victims, that is to say, as victims themselves.

Now that so many individuals and "communities" vie for victim status by turning their past sufferings into the pillars of their identity, we should pay special attention to the Amalek syndrome. It is a threat to people, to families and to nations. Amalek awakes whenever we hear the scream of resentment for past ills, whenever rancour persuades us that memory grants more rights than duties.

That scream is what the Bible warns us against in the paradoxical injunction quoted above: "Remember what Amalek did to you on your journey . . . You shall blot out the memory of Amalek from under heaven. Do not forget!" (Deuteronomy 25:17–19).

Is there a way of remembering whilst blotting out memory? Human resilience may indeed depend on that subtle commandment: remember what happened to you;

be sure to keep the memory of the past; but do not allow that past to scream in your head in the voice of Amalek. Don't allow hatred—the hatred that struck you down, or the hatred that possessed you—to dictate your whole identity. It's not a matter of silencing the voices of our inheritance or past sufferings, but of not allowing them the sole right of speech in our minds, as if they alone accounted for what we can be.

"An hairy man": The story of Esau

Going backwards in time along a biblical path from the Persia of Haman to Amalek's battle in the desert, the rabbis' pursuit takes us further still.

Who was the grandfather in the family of Jew-haters? Esau. As you might expect, he is no stranger to the story of his descendants and their obsessions.

Esau's complex destiny began in his mother's womb, in a fight that took place *in utero*. Two foetuses jostled inside the body of a woman called Rebeka: "the children struggled in her womb" (Genesis 25:22). This is the first biblical pregnancy that did not go well. The woman with child turned to God and asked: "If so, why do I exist?" (Genesis 25:22). That is the expression of the existential crisis of a woman torn apart by the conflict that rages inside her.

Jacob and Esau are twins and enemies before they are born. According to rabbinical commentaries, they are on opposite sides from the moment of conception. There are legends that attribute to them unbelievable struggles over territory and theology whilst still in their mother's womb. One such says that whenever Rebeka walked past a synagogue, Jacob jiggled around inside her, trying to get out to go to pray. Whenever she walked past an idolatrous temple, however, Esau was just as active (Bereishit Rabbah 63:3).

The anecdote is as anachronistic as it is unrealistic— there were no synagogues in biblical times, nor were there any ultrasound scans! However, in the rabbis' minds, the story gave a contemporary setting to the opposition between the two worlds that the brothers embody: Judaism and idolatry came from the same amniotic sac.

Esau's hatred of Jacob is presented in rabbinical writings as if it were a law, an unalterable and imponderable truth: "Rejoice in the law (*halakha*): Esau hates Jacob" (Midrash Sifrei, Bealoth'a 9).

Starting from this passage in the Bible, the twin brother Esau turns into an emblem of anti-Jewish hatred and the hostile principle that accompanies the very birth of the people of Israel, as if Jews and their enemies could only arise together at the same point in time. Why should hatred and its object come from the same womb? Why should anti-Semitism be presented as a family affair?

39

Jacob and Esau have a common lineage, a common inheritance, a common history and origin. And it was specifically over their inheritance that they fought all their lives long. The Bible gives the full detail of their struggles to keep or to grasp the status of the first-born, a status that offered the higher blessing, as if there were not enough room in the world or in that family for two blessings of equal value.

Jacob is the winner: he swaps that famous plate of lentils for his brother's privilege, then usurps his father's blessing by pretending to be Esau. Cunning, not force, wins out again and again in the battle of the brothers.

Physical force is Esau's thing. He is said to be a hunter and a strong man, and, surprisingly, to have been born "an hairy man" (Genesis 27:11). (Later on, this feature links him to the biblical land of Seir—literally, the land of the hairy—whence came Timna.) By being born with a lot of hair, it is as if Esau were already virile at birth, a grown man before passing through puberty.

Jacob, on the other hand, is said to be a "smooth man" (Genesis 27:11)—a mother's boy and her favourite, clinging to her skirts and cooking in the tent.

The conflict of the twins is presented from the start as a competition between two archetypes, as if it were a conflict of civilisations tacked onto a war between genders. On one side, the virile Esau, and on the other, Jacob, with his more effeminate qualities. It's almost a declaration of the war of sexes. This recurs time and again in anti-Semitic rhetoric when Jews are described as "womanish", unmanly and hysterical. We will come back to this point.

Esau's world is already fully composed, already created, so to speak (in Hebrew his name means "already done"). Jacob's Hebrew name, YAAKOV, however, is a verb in the future tense meaning "he will be on the heel". As Jacob came into the world holding his brother's heel, his name effectively says "he will follow". He has not yet arrived; he is not yet "made". He is "to be continued . . ."

The rest of the story tells us how that worked out. One day, Jacob acquired another name: Israel. For the time being, however, he is the one who is "not yet". He is the figure of a potential existence as yet unrealised; he is, so to speak, a "perhaps". The struggle between the two brothers is, in the last analysis, the war between the complete and the incomplete that has been fought since the beginning of time. Esau would like to overcome Jacob: the world of the finite would very much like to get rid of "perhaps". Two kinds of civilisation stand set against each other in the brothers' struggle: totality versus infinity.

Let us pause in our investigation of the genealogy of hatred from its beginnings and look at the clues we have gathered. Anti-Semites arise in the Bible as soon as Jews do. They seem to have sprung from the same womb, or the same verse. Right from the start the one reproaches the other for splitting off, for being different.

They are not wrong: Jewish identity is grounded in separation.

In the first place, Jews had the cheek to separate from their origins and to maintain at all times that they were not identical to their place of birth. Under each of their names, their definition is a setting-off for somewhere else, and non-equivalence to themselves. This identity appears to be forever stepping to one side, instead of seeking to be "at one" with the group or its origin, as all other people do.

That's exactly what Haman says in his hatred of Jews. He asks: "Why should they be apart?" Whilst they are around, he tells the king, "There will be no equality among the rest of us." In other words: as long as Jews remain apart, we won't have all *our* part. For if they remove themselves from the common lot, then they confiscate our potential to be fully ourselves, to be completely at one in our nation or with ourselves.

Haman's forebear Amalek inherited the same language

and the same suffering from long before, from the womb that gave him birth. Son of a sexually abused girl or else of a rejected mother, depending on which of the legends you believe, Amalek is in either case the heir to a pain that turns into hatred. For him, the Hebrews were those folk who prevented him from being what he could have been in the place he should have had. He finds himself named "without a people", and this amputation spurs him on like an obsession to destroy whosoever in his eyes embodies belonging.

Amalek's grandfather Esau had experienced the same thing. He was convinced that his own share had been stolen, that the inheritance that was his by right had been grabbed by his brother. His world yearns for finiteness and wholeness, whereas his brother represents the infinite potential of becoming, the world of "perhaps". How could he allow his twin brother Jacob, whose origin was the same as his, to carry off that inheritance to some other place?

However far they take them, the rabbis' investigations all lead back to a single scenario: in the Scriptures, Jew-hatred always derives from a conflicted rapport with origin, from an inheritance and from ancestral resentment. It is always an expression of jealousy within a family, of a rivalry between brothers or cousins that leaves the hater unable to recover, or of such envy that the hater wishes the other to cease living.

It is the kind of hatred that constantly asks: *why has my brother got what was not given to me?* Why does he have a right of seniority that casts me into the second, unfavoured position? It matters little whether the injustice is real or imagined, or whether the hater has come across actual Jews or not: Jew-hatred gives form to a sense of inadequacy.

Convincing themselves that the other has not yet ceased to be or persists in becoming, anti-Semites end up believing that Jews are and always will be "more" than they are. How can they bear the Jews being both the ones who came before and the ones who go beyond them? That really is too much . . .

CHAPTER TWO

Anti-Semitism Is a Clash of Civilisations

One day a Jew walked past Emperor Hadrian. The Jew uttered a respectful salutation.

"Who are you?" the emperor asked.

"I'm a Jew," the man replied.

"How dare you speak to me?!" the emperor shouted, and gave an order for the man to be hanged.

A second Jew walked past, but he did not salute Hadrian.

"Who are you?" the emperor asked.

"I'm a Jew," the man replied.

"How dare you not salute me?!" the emperor shouted, and gave an order for the man to be hanged.

The emperor's counsellor asked the emperor what his logic was, and Hadrian replied:

"Are you trying to tell me how to get rid of my enemies?"
[Midrash Eichah Rabbah 3:41; sixth century CE]

Early rabbinical writings point out the obvious absurdity and irrationality of the motive for anti-Semitism. They often depict it with the sour humour of resignation.

45

If the hatred of Jews has no logical grounds, then it would perhaps be quite pointless or even immoral to look for ways of explaining it, or to try to analyse the reasoning of its propagators. It would certainly be useless unless we also ask what precisely it is that the hater hates in Jews, and what it is that his hatred denotes. Who or what is the enemy that anti-Semites must be rid of?

An empirical experiment

In rabbinical writings of the early centuries of the Common Era, the Roman Empire is frequently given as a motive for anti-Semitism, and it can be considered a central topic. There's nothing surprising about that. At the time when the Talmud was being put together, Jews lived under the sway of Rome. They were at the mercy of Rome's power and administration. That's why Rome is the very figure of dominance: a power that controls everything, which can grant you prosperity or else take your life.

This reality is particularly significant after the destruction of the Second Temple in Jerusalem in 70 CE. Lacking sovereignty over any lands and henceforth deprived of a central religious institution, rabbinical Judaism came to replace the priestly form of the faith as the basic organisation of the Jewish community. Little by little, it was adopted by an entire population and became the hegemonic structure of their society. This form of Judaism made the Book its central religious institution and saw interpretation of Scripture as a new terrain for encountering the divine.

There are stories offering different models for collaborating with Roman authorities after the destruction of the Temple, as well as for more or less violent opposition to them. Some of these tales are clearly fictitious, whilst others are based on real events. Among the best known of these stories is one about the struggle for Massada. A group of Jewish rebels took refuge in a fortress at the top of a mountain in Judea and stood firm against a Roman legion. After a siege lasting several months in 73 CE, the rebels chose to kill themselves rather than yield Massada to the Empire. It's the emblematic story of Jewish resistance of the most extreme kind, of self-sacrifice preferred to any kind of compromise with the enemy.

However, the rabbis of the early centuries—the people who were writing down the Judaism that we have inherited—distance themselves very sharply from this story and the ideology it represents. The models they praise are not fortresses defended to the last man. On the contrary, they take quite different figures from the Talmud as their heroes, including the legendary Yohanan ben Zakkai. He was a spiritual leader in Jerusalem in 70 CE, who realised that the Temple would fall and got himself out of the city by pretending to be dead. Ben Zakkai escaped from the siege and went out of the walled city of David in a coffin carried by his disciples.

The dead man, who wasn't dead at all, approached the commander of the Roman legions, a man called Vespasian, and managed to extract a favour from him. "Give me Yavne and its sages and do not destroy it," he pleaded (Talmud Gittin 56b). That was how he founded a study room and a rabbinical court. These two institutions became the key centres of Jewish thought as it reconstructed itself. Elie Wiesel wondered why he asked for Yavne. "Not as a replacement for Jerusalem: Jerusalem would remain irreplaceable for ever. But so as to be able to dream of Jerusalem, outside Jerusalem. So as to live by the Law in a different way from before. To learn, or to relearn how to live in waiting."[4]

The story is, of course, a legend, but this literary fiction does symbolise a kind of Judaism that rises from the embers without seeking to replace what was destroyed, and thus creates a new condition for religious expectation, which is the heart of rabbinical Jewish thought in the period of (re)construction.

The destruction of the Temple and the coffin of Rabbi Yohanan ben Zakkai seem on first reading to narrate the death and final end of Judaism. In fact, they hide the turn

4 Elie Wiesel, *Célébration talmudique* (Paris: Seuil, 1991), p. 56.

that it took at this point in the history of the Jews. A religious system based on sacrifice and a physical location was transformed into a relationship to Scripture that was experienced as if it were a "portable nation", in Daniel Boyarin's phrase, and a culture of learning and patient adaptation. In the eyes of the sages, choosing political compromise and making a theological revolution had an obvious cost—recognition of the Jews' dependence on the authorities, since there was no alternative. The rabbis of Yavne were perfectly aware that their religious plans depended on the goodwill of the Roman Empire. The connection with Rome and its local representatives thus became the central subject of rabbinical writings.[5] The relationship with power remained a main topic of Jewish thought over the following centuries, since the survival of Jews has always depended on secular authorities.

The hands of Esau and the acts of Rome

Very soon after the destruction of the Temple, there appears in rabbinical writing an expression used so often that it becomes a code. From the early second century CE,

5 Danny Trom, in *Persévérance du fait juif* (Paris: ÉHÉSS/Gallimard/Seuil, 2018), suggests seeing the State of Israel as an "externalisation", or substitute, for the nations and empires that failed to look after Jews.

Romans are reputed to be "children of Esau"; in the Talmud, that phrase comes to be a way of referring to the Roman Empire.[6]

By making their oppressors the reincarnation of Esau, the rabbis seem to transpose to first-century Judea the legend of Romulus and Remus, the twin brothers who founded Rome. That also makes Jews and Romans fratricidal brothers. So why did the rabbis choose to characterise their enemy as a biblical character who is none other than their own ancestral twin?

Perhaps it was in order to use the Scripture as a hint of a coming liberation. In the Bible, Esau's father does promise him a kingdom, but the Scripture also dooms the son to an inescapable fall. If you see the power of Rome as the realisation of an ancient prophecy made in the Bible, then you also believe it will come crashing down one day.

But we could also take the analogy of Esau and Rome as a much vaster metaphor. If Jews and Romans are enemies from the womb, then we would have to believe that their opposition is not incidental, but essential. To describe Roman and Jewish civilisations as brothers who are enemies of each other is a way of asserting that their antagonism is eternal, and to ground it in two opposing types of humanity that were in conflict even in the womb.

6 Mireille Hadas-Lebel, "Jacob et Esaü ou Israël et Rome dans le Talmud et le Midrash", *Revue de l'histoire des religions* 201:4 (1984), pp. 369–92.

Esau's hatred of Jacob would then be like a war of civilisations: not a territorial or political enmity, but rather rancour for an antagonistic way of being in the world. On this view, Rome would take Jews as the almost exclusive object of its resentment; what's more, that hatred would be part of the very foundation of Roman civilisation. At least, that is the thought that a famous passage in the Talmud invites us to entertain.

The rabbi and the emperor

The Talmudic treatise known as Avodah Zarah tells the story of a surprising friendship between an emperor and a rabbi. Once upon a time there was a Roman aristocrat who dreamed of befriending a sage . . . It begins like a lovable and really implausible fairy story. Historically speaking, it is quite unrealistic. It is not conceivable that a highly placed imperial subject would become closely acquainted with a mere Jewish teacher.

Many written sources provide unambiguous evidence that Roman traditions were shot through with hatred and scorn for Jews. On several occasions the legions of the Roman army crushed rebellions by religious minorities in the provinces of the Empire, and Jews were not exempt from this regular policy. The most famous of the Jewish uprisings, the Bar Kokhba revolt in the second century CE, was put down with bloody violence.

All the same, many Talmudic passages portray friendly or teasing relations between the two sides in the form of good-hearted discussions and debates between Roman leaders and Jews. Some of them portray an emperor or a general wanting to learn the keys to Israel's wisdom, rituals and longevity.

A Roman world making nice with a Jewish world: what this imaginary alternative to historical power relations shows us above all is the fantasy world of a community under siege, and the power of imagination to make up for political impotence. "Let's imagine a world where Rome would come and take counsel from us" is what these tales ask us to hear.

That's how this fictional narrative arose, but its value does not lie just in the comfort it gave its creators and readers. It also contains, here and there, a treatise on political philosophy, and a cunning exploration of the imagined mind of the adversary.

The oral tradition of Jewish law that was first written down between the second and sixth century CE has been compared by many scholars to an ocean. You can swim through it under water, but you must remain aware that it has untold depths that can only be explored with humility. Let us step into those waters until we lose our footing . . .

The King and I (Talmudic version)

We are on the shore of a famous episode in the ocean of the Talmud. The scene is taken from the Avodah Zarah, meaning "foreign worship" (or "idolatry"), and it deals with the Jews' encounter with idolaters, which is how the rabbis saw the Romans and their emperor. The hero of the passage is a rabbi called Yehuda HaNasi, or Judah the Prince. He was one of the main authors of the first written version of the oral law (the Mishnah) in the second century CE. He was such a giant of learning that he is referred to in the texts simply as "Master". When the word "Rabbi" is used without a supplementary name of a wise man, it means Judah the Prince.

The passage we are dealing with describes the connection between Rabbi and the Roman emperor of the time, Antoninus, who may perhaps have been Antoninus Pius (86–161 CE), the father of Marcus Aurelius Severus. Here is how the story begins:

> Every day Antoninus would minister to Rabbi Yehuda HaNasi; he would feed him and give him to drink. When Rabbi Yehuda HaNasi wanted to ascend to his bed, Antoninus would bend down in front of the bed and say to him: Ascend upon me to your bed. Rabbi Yehuda HaNasi said in response: It is not proper

conduct to treat the king with this much disrespect. Antoninus said: Oh, that I were set as a mattress under you in the World-to-Come! [Avodah Zarah 10b]

Act 1: In the rabbi's bedchamber

The opening lines of this passage from the Talmud sound like a weird joke. They exploit and mock everything the Jews are so often accused of: wanting to rule the world, to corrupt the powerful, to bring them to their knees and to walk right over them. The circumstances depicted look like a humorous rabbinical fantasy and an admission of powerlessness. As is often the case, the fiction provides consolation to those in no position to experience it, and expresses the dream of a complete reversal of real-world roles. The story appears to ask: if the great emperor, the political master of the whole empire, were to put himself at the service of one of our folk, then what would we do with him?

Many details are given of Antoninus' submission and not one of them is without meaning: he gives his master food and drink, acts as a footstool to help him climb into bed, and dreams of being trampled on in the world to come, that is to say, for all eternity.

For the well-informed reader of the Talmud, these images are very suggestive. They paint a picture of a specific kind of servitude that is almost sexual in nature. For example, in another Talmudic treatise these specific domestic tasks (pouring drink, making the bed) are those that a wife does for her husband, in full awareness that she could thereby arouse irrepressible desire in him. The Talmud also contains descriptions of the sexual act where the woman is likened to a mattress for her husband (Babylonian Talmud, Ketubot 61a, 96a; Eruvin 100b; Yevamot 62b), as if she might serve as a "stepping stone" into the next world for him. Such metaphors, drawn from the patriarchal world from which these treatises come, lead Daniel Boyarin to judge that Antoninus' services to the Rabbi play on all the literary strings of erotic tension.[7] The relationship between the two men is presented all of a sudden as something resembling marriage, and desire plays a key role in it.

By taking on such domestic tasks the emperor turned himself, in a sense, into the sage's wife. He became a devoted and submissive spouse. In the patriarchal world of the Jews and the Romans, this allegory has a meaning: it constitutes a reversal of master and slave, and increases the implausible and imaginary nature of the whole story. In this literary world, virility attaches to the rabbis, but in

7   Daniel Boyarin, "Homotopia: The Feminized Jewish Man and the Lives of Women in Late Antiquity", *Differences: A Journal of Feminist Cultural Criticism* 7:2 (summer 1995), p. 41.

the real world, it is unarguably attached to the Empire and its head, the alpha male of the dominant culture. We will come back to this point.

The conversation between Judah the Prince and the emperor then takes an even more surprising turn, and veers from the domestic sphere to the theological.

> Antoninus said to Rabbi Yehuda HaNasi: Will I enter the World-to-Come?
> Rabbi Yehuda HaNasi said to him: Yes.
> Antoninus said to him: But isn't it written: "And there shall not be any remaining of the house of Esau" [Obadiah 1:18]?
> Rabbi Yehuda HaNasi answered: The verse is stated with regard to those who perform actions similar to those of the wicked Esau, not to people like you.
> . . . The inference learned from the wording of the verse . . . serves to exclude Antoninus the son of Asveirus . . . and the Roman officer Ketia, son of Shalom. [Avodah Zarah 10b]

Act 2: In the rabbi's study area

Suddenly it seems that the protagonists have left the rabbi's bedroom and their conjugal relationship, and are now in another room of the house: the courtyard of the study area, where exegesis, the tradition of interpreting Scripture, was practised. The discussion between the emperor and the wise man steps into terrain appropriate to the great debates of the rabbinical schools.

Here too the words spoken are implausible. Why would a Roman leader be bothered to know whether he had a place in the world to come, that is to say, after the Day of Judgment, by a Creator he didn't believe in? Yet the great emperor wonders: do salvation and redemption exist for me (and for my pagan world), or will I forever remain in error and irredeemable confusion?

The rabbi tries to reassure him, but he cannot, because the emperor of this imaginary tale knows the sources better than the Jewish wise man does. He finds textual proof of the impossibility of his being redeemed and of his irreversible damnation in a line in the Bible, from the book of the prophet Obadiah. "But isn't it written," he asks, "'And there shall not be any remaining of the house of Esau'?" So here an idolater cites Jewish Scripture entirely accurately and, by appealing to the Prophets, he adopts the language and cultural references of his adversary as if it were a normal thing to do. Literature allows us to investigate what such reversals of norms and power relations might mean.

At the start of the passage, the men are manly no more and the smart guy is not the one you would expect. It doesn't make sense—except with respect to the question that the rabbis pretend to put in the mouth of another. The moral and religious question can be stated in this way: are our enemies irrecoverably and definitively evil, or do they have a path to salvation? Are they damned from birth and by nature, or can they redeem themselves? Can hatred of Jews be cast out, or does it define for all eternity the world and the culture that is theirs? Or, to put it in the style of biblical filiation: can Esau's world act in a different way from its ancestor?

The rabbi's answer: nothing is settled! The sentence afflicts not Esau's descendants, but "those who perform actions similar to those of the wicked Esau". Hatred of Jews is therefore not part of the nature of Rome, it just happens to be present in Rome. The sage is suggesting that the anti-Jewish hatred that was supported by the paganism of those times is not inescapable, provided it succeeds in not "performing actions like those of Esau".

What then are the actions "like those of Esau" which must be avoided? What does it mean to cast them out? That's what the remainder of this Talmudic tale tries to clarify by taking a detour into another episode that is subtly connected to it and that sheds new light on it. The conversation goes on: "Not all Romans behave like Esau. There are exceptions: such as you, Antoninus, or Ketia son of Shalom."

Who was Ketia?

Another story and another hero suddenly turn up in the Talmud. An unknown man called Ketia son of Shalom arises. Apparently a member of an older generation, Ketia is presented by the story as a key to understanding the debate between the emperor and the rabbi. *So who was Ketia son of Shalom?* is the question asked by the continuation of the episode, as if a byway through another tale was required, just like in the *Thousand and One Nights*.

> As there was a certain Roman emperor who hated the Jews he said to the important members of the kingdom: If one had an ulcerous sore rise on his foot, should he cut it off and live, or leave it and suffer? They said to him: He should cut it off and live. [Avodah Zara 10b]

Act 3: In the emperor's army

After the emperor who loved Jews, now we have one who hated them. The identity of this second Roman leader is not stated, but he is much more in keeping with the image of Roman power that the Talmudic rabbis give us than Antoninus is, and much closer to their actual experience of imperial rule. He doesn't offer to be stepped on by the people of Judea; on the contrary, he rules over them without mercy.

59

One day this emperor speaks to his henchmen and counsellors and asks them an allegorical question: what should be done to damaged skin with a wound and a sore that threaten to infect an otherwise healthy body?

The physical and medical metaphor has a clear meaning. It's one cherished by anti-Semites of all eras and it has been repeated a thousand times: Jews are a source of contamination for the body of their host and a threat to its integrity. They are accused of breaking the continuity of the social body and of being parasites in the land that accepts them. Jews, like ulcers, cause a breach in the body; in other words, they are responsible for the breakdown of the society that accepts them. That's where the phrase "dirty Jew" comes from—to make it clear that the presence of Jews pollutes and weakens the host. They are a source of pathogens.

The argument slips very quickly into a different register. Initially accused of fostering contamination, Jews then become the contamination itself. Jews are an infectious agent, the "racial tuberculosis of the nations" according to Hitler,[8] a harmful animal poisoning the land: vermin, fleas, bloodsucking insects gnawing the flesh to destruction, making the body unable to protect itself from the foreign body that penetrates it and causes it to fall apart. In

8 Letter to Gemlich, 1919, in *Hitler: Sämtliche Aufzeichnungen 1905–1924*, ed. Eberhard Jäckel (Stuttgart: Deutsche Verlagsanstalt, 1980), pp. 88–90.

October 2018, at a meeting in Detroit that was recorded and then posted on social media, Louis Farrakhan, the leader of the Nation of Islam, compared Jews to insects eating the nation away and stated: "I am not an anti-Semite, I am anti-Termite."[9]

Wholeness is always the issue. *Anti-Semites of every age have always been partisans of wholeness.* They believe Jews make holes in membranes or in worlds, that by creating hybrids and mixtures they are a threat to territorial borders, national identities, family unity. In their eyes, Jews are what make clear lines impossible, because they cloud things over, undermine them or violate them. Jews make holes and sores.

> Jews are not another group or members of another group. They belong to a group in the way that patho-genic organs may belong to a body that it infects or threatens to infect. Jews are agents of an auto-immune deficiency: they turn against the immunity of the very body to which they belong.[10]

"What can we do to protect the integrity of the nation and the Empire?" the hateful emperor asks his counsellors,

9   Rosa Doherty, "Louis Farrakhan keeps his Twitter account", *Jewish Chronicle*, October 18, 2018.
10 Jean-Luc Nancy, *Exclu le juif en nous* (Paris: Galilée, 2018), p. 25.

appealing to their conscience. Must we cut off the spreader of sores, or else live in pain with the hole? Should we block up the sore by getting rid of the gap, or live painfully with an open wound?

When the question was put in that way with the support of a bloody image, the counsellors came up with an answer in double-quick time: cut out the ulcer to save your life! There's only one solution: amputate!

Let's cut ourselves off from the people who embody discontinuity, they say with one voice, unaware of the obvious contradiction that such an answer leaves hanging: how can you cut off a gap or amputate an absence? None of them grasp the point—save one.

One man alone sees how absurd the proposal is. He's called Ketia Bar Shalom, and he's about to come into the text and step onto the stage of history.

Ketia, son of Shalom, said [to the counsellors]: It is unwise to do so, for two reasons. One is that you cannot destroy all of them. [Avodah Zarah 10b]

Act 4: Inside a man's head

For a counsellor who is not Jewish, the man has a funny-sounding name—not a Latin one, at any rate. Is he a Jew? Probably not, otherwise a Jew-hating emperor could hardly have given him the job that he has. So why does the Talmud call him "Bar Shalom"? Maybe it's a pseudonym—not one adopted by the man, but given to him by the scribes of the Talmud to say what sort of a man he was and to suggest how subtly he would gainsay the emperor.

Word for word, "Ketia Bar Shalom" means "the cut (*Ketia*), son of or coming from (*Bar*) peace or wholeness (*Shalom*)".

So the man called "Disconnect coming from Wholeness" steps out from among the soldiers of Rome, and the name he is given all but announces what he's going to do next: to break with his identity group. That's the sole substance of his words as soon as he opens his mouth.

He starts his demonstration by saying *Ch'ada*, "In the first place . . ."—but the expression also means "sharp-edged" like a blade, and therefore able to cut off anything at a stroke. "In the first place, you will never be able to cut yourselves off from the Jews entirely." So what Ketia tells the emperor is that first of all you will never recover your wholeness, the Oneness you dream of, by cutting them off; nor will getting rid of them restore you to the state of purity you fantasise about.

In saying this, by arguing that cutting off the Jews is impossible, Ketia is cutting himself off from his comrades.

Then he quotes a verse from the Bible in support of his argument:

For it is written: "For I have spread you abroad as the four winds of the heaven, says the Lord" [Zechariah 2:10] . . . Just as the world cannot exist without winds, so too, the world cannot exist without the Jewish people . . . And furthermore, if you attempt to carry out the destruction of the Jews, they will call you the severed kingdom. [Avodah Zarah 10b]

As when Antoninus cited the Prophets earlier on in this passage, Ketia's speech is quite implausible. It's most unlikely any imperial counsellor ever attempted to win over a pagan leader by quoting from Jewish Scripture or invoking a prophet. Roman eloquence was made of different stuff!

However, the argument itself goes off on a strange tack—to the wind. "You'll never get rid of the people of Israel," Ketia tells the emperor, "because they are like the wind." Meaning? Nobody can hold the wind, catch it, stop it or get rid of it. It is impalpable and invisible, and can only be identified from the movement it causes. Moreover, the world could not exist without it.

Ketia's line lies halfway between classical anti-Semitic rhetoric (they get everywhere, they're invisible, they're infiltrators pulling all the strings . . .) and an unconditional defence of the Jews, whose Scriptures tell the truth and without whom the world would collapse.

"And what's more, they'll call *you* the severed kingdom!"

The key to Ketia Bar Shalom's whole intervention could well be contained in that sentence. In only a few words, he makes the emperor face his own contradiction. Can the Empire allow itself to appear cut off? On the other hand, can it allow the cut-off to live on inside it? The answer is straightforward, and comes from a principle of Roman rule: the unity of the Empire's territory. That was the basis of Pax Romana, "the peace of Rome". As the Empire expanded, it imposed its laws and jurisdiction over lands that it unified. Rome was the world of *pax*, that is to say, of *shalom*, of which the literal meaning is "wholeness". It was an empire of continuity and plenitude.

Now, out of hatred for Jews, an emperor wants to sever himself in order to restore legendary unity. So Ketia asks him: do you really think you can make your land into a severed kingdom (*Ketia* meaning "severed") so as to protect your integrity and identity?

This question is a cover for the deeper issue of the confrontation between Rome and the Jews. By extension, the rabbis take it as an expression of the underlying problem of anti-Jewish hate. Jews are the embodiment of the impossibility of the uniform expansion of the Empire.

Jean-Luc Nancy has described the stand-off in this way: historically, Jews were perceived as obstacles to the expansion of the Empire and its control of the known world, or as enemies of a "fine and healthy alliance of nations".

What distinguishes anti-Semitism from all other kinds of racism is that it attributes to or invents in "the Jew" a figure that contains all the obstacles to the spread of power. In this respect anti-Semitic hostility is far removed from racist hostility. It has less to do with relations between groups than with a relationship to the self and with a kind of power that aims to reign over all groups.[11]

In this way of thinking, anti-Semitism is the desire of a person, a group or an empire to exterminate an internal feature that undermines its own expansion. Jews are not external "others" blocking unfettered expansion, but internal blocks that cause ulceration and prevent the body from growing larger or from being whole.

Jews, seen as separate beings within the collective body, prevent the kingdom or the nation or the family from being "One" or from achieving "totality". It's as if their very presence were a constant reminder of the impossibility of wholeness.

That is why Jews are believed to be capable of making borders porous and of introducing or creating fractures in society. A white supremacist who opened fire on worshippers at a synagogue in Pittsburgh on October 27, 2018 was

11 Nancy, *Exclu le juif en nous*, pp. 29–30.

motivated by the same argument: in his posts, he accused Jews of aiding members of Central American caravans moving towards the United States border and of "bringing invaders in that kill our people". Jews obstruct *shalom* and national unity and thereby act as unwelcome reminders of the absence that has to be suffered in living. In short, Jews are cut off and remind us of everything else in our world that is similarly unmoored. So to sever the severed, you turn them into the cause of it all.

And the culprits will have to pay for it.

The story of Ketia Bar Shalom and his place in Scripture are summed up in the man's name: "cut-off arising from wholeness".

He was born in a world that cherished completeness. All the same, he succeeded in confronting the emperor with the gap in himself. That's what made him an ideal culprit. The story continues:

> The emperor said to Ketia: You have spoken well and your statement is correct; but they throw anyone who defeats the king in argument into a house full of ashes where he would die. [Avodah Zarah 10b]

Act 5: Violence is unleashed

The man of power is humbled by his counsellor's argument, which lays bare the weaknesses in his own position and identity. Can an emperor cope with such a wound to his ego without falling apart? Your demonstration is excellent, the ruler grants—but what right do you have to tie me in knots? Who dares get the better of me has a price to pay! The servant's intellectual mastery of his master could be likened to a symbolic castration, which was quite unacceptable to the imperial regime. Whoever impugns its honour has to disappear entirely and be turned to dust and ashes. What is at stake is the integrity of the ruler, and therefore of the realm.

Ketia is going to be thrown into a fire pit. It's not an arbitrary reference for the rabbis of the Midrash. Abraham, the father of monotheism, he who gave up idol worship, had to suffer the same trial in childhood when he was thrown into a fire by Nimrod the tyrant of Chaldea, and by a miracle survived unhurt. It's as if Ketia was turning into a son of Abraham through a symbolic repetition of the same initiation ritual.

When they were seizing Ketia and going to take him to his death, a certain matron said to him: Woe to the ship that goes without paying the tax. Ketia bent down over his foreskin, severed it, and said: I gave my tax; I will pass and enter. [Avodah Zarah 10b]

Suddenly we hear the voice of a woman, a Roman matron, in this tale. The text seems to require an outside witness, the voice of another, as it happens a female voice, to play the role of the Other. She is the third party to the story. In the Talmud, women quite often provide that external voice of wisdom challenging dominant power, and male dominance more generally. The physical and political powerlessness of women is the key to that other power which comes from everyday words and deeds.

The role of women in the Talmud is always to provide the insight of an outsider. In that respect, women and Jews are strangely connected. Both groups are equally powerless in a world dominated by Rome, and can only act politically with the tools that they have: verbal cunning and verbal seduction.

Language is the weapon of women and Jews in the Scriptures. The power of a word or phrase is called *mila* in Hebrew, but that is an ambiguous term, since it can also refer to circumcision. In Hebrew, *mila* is a severance made either in an expression or in a body. It makes a gap, creates discontinuity. Because of his words and the power of his speech Ketia is severed from his own people and thrown into the other world. But can he really go there? Will it be easy to withdraw him from a world obsessed with whole-ness, the one which saw him born and grown?

The matron addresses him to ask, in the coded speech of myth: can a ship pass without paying the tax?

The ship obviously harks back to the Greek and then Roman myth of Charon, who ferried the dead to the under-world across the River Styx (meaning "hate"). What the matron asks is: can Ketia cross the hatred without paying his fare?

In rabbinical minds the question is also a near perfect match for the question put to Yehuda HaNasi a few lines earlier by Emperor Antoninus: "Will I enter the World-to-Come?" To put it another way: is it possible for a child of Esau, who belongs to an idolatrous nation, to escape from the hatred she harbours and to cross over into another mental world?

Straight away, Ketia, the man of severance, tears off his foreskin, copying Abraham's act of circumcision. "Those who pay the fare may pass." Yes, Ketia asserts, the hatred can pass out of me. But there is a price. The cost is to cut something off and to choose to live in incompleteness.

However, Ketia's circumcision was not a conversion, strictly speaking. The Roman counsellor did not become a Jew in that instant. However, the physical severance completes a process that began well before, with the words that he spoke. Ketia had cut himself off from the mind of his anti-Semitic master and its obsession with wholeness, and he left it for a journey far from his place of origin, just as Abraham once did, to espouse separation and to abandon the worship of completeness. Ketia had become not a Jew, but a child of Abraham, and to some degree a non-idolater like Abraham, who was the first of them all. He'd turned into an *ivri* in the original sense of the word: a passer-by who can now pass over . . .

How can we fit the two parts of this story together?

On the one hand, there's an emperor prepared to become feminine insofar as his relation to the world of the Jews is concerned. On the other hand, there's a sovereign not at all inclined to let himself be castrated by the presence of Jews who threaten his integrity or by the arguments of a counsellor who cuts himself off, and cuts off a part of his body, too.

Antoninus and Ketia are both said to have a place in the World-to-Come: which is to say, they can free themselves from the murderous hate that is destroying a part of their own people. The possibility that sons of Esau do not have to act like Esau—that they have the capacity to cast off inherited anti-Semitism—is clearly stated, but is also made dependent on specific behaviour, namely, the ability to live with severance, fracture and incompleteness, and the strength to resist the temptation of wholeness.

In Jewish thought the ability to live with an unbounded

absence is called "the feminine" and in Hebrew the word used is NEKEVA, which has the literal meaning of "hole" or "obliteration". In our story it is related through the feminine side of an emperor in his almost conjugal relationship to his teacher, and through the feminine character of a matron offering a passage to a man condemned to death by the emperor, or again through an imperial counsellor whose self-circumcision speaks of his cutting himself off from his origins.

Neither Antoninus nor Ketia converts to Judaism. Judaism makes no claim that there is no salvation outside of its own faith. However, rabbinical thinking seems to ask us to be wary of the threat to any identity that considers itself entire, namely, the hatred of Jews for being the external form of the fracture that people refuse to acknowledge in themselves.

You don't have to be a Jew to live with something missing. But it's hard not to be anti-Semitic when what you want above all else is to live without void and without fracture.

Castration

Let us leave off from our enquiry into the Talmud and take a great leap through time and space from the first centuries of the Common Era in the Roman province of Judea to the early years of the twentieth century in central Europe.

In Vienna, in 1909, Sigmund Freud puzzled over little Hans, a five-year-old boy who suffered from irrational fears. In the essay that he wrote on the case, the inventor of psychoanalysis added a stunning footnote: "The castration complex is the deepest unconscious root of anti-Semitism." He adds: "And there is no stronger unconscious root for the sense of superiority over women."[12]

A century ago Freud established a direct connection between anti-Semitism and misogyny as emanations of a common mental landscape, coming from the same depths of the unconscious, and from a fear of castration, that is to say, of the void, of loss and separation. When the Other embodies lack and the impossibility of wholeness, we hate him for threatening our own wholeness. We deeply resent the fracture made in our own sense of completeness.

Hadn't the Talmud been there before in its description of the conflict with Rome? The sages hint many times that hatred of Jews cannot be grasped without thinking about the place of womanhood in Scripture and in history. Because, in the eye of the hater, Jews and women are but two different manifestations of incompleteness.

Long before that, the Bible had already given a foretaste

12 Sigmund Freud, "Analysis of a Phobia in a Five-Year-Old Boy: 'Little Hans'", in *The Standard Edition of the Complete Psychological Works of Sigmund Freud*, ed. and trans. James Strachey, vol. 10 (London: Hogarth, 1955), p. 198.

of the argument in a book we have already mentioned, the book of Esther. In this episode the topics of castration and anti-Semitism appear simultaneously. Haman, the enemy of the Jews, ardently wants to wipe them all out, and he instigates a genocide in the palace of a sovereign named Assuerus, all of whose servants, according to the text, are . . . eunuchs. The castration of all the men in the king's service recurs like a leitmotiv throughout the book of Esther, to a comical degree: what kind of a kingdom can that be if almost all the men are physically as well as politically impotent?

It is a kingdom ruled by virulent misogyny. Near the start of the tale, the king promises his subjects that every man will soon be respected once again by his wife and "wield authority in his home" (Esther 1:22). In the palace of the king of Persia, castrating servants protects the women's quarters (the *gynaeceum*), yet it is precisely amidst impotence and threatened virility that anti-Semitism emerges and unleashes its mad fury.

Possibly making a subtle allusion to this source, the Talmud, first written down several hundred years later, tells the story of Emperor Antoninus and refers to him as "Antoninus son of Severus" . . . but, believe it or not, when the Talmudic scribe wrote that name down, he made a spelling mistake. He added the letter *aleph*, which sounds like an "A", at the start of the name of the emperor. So

74

whereas the Rabbi addressed himself to "Antoninus son of Severus", we read "son of Assuerus".

Whenever anti-Semitism pokes its nose out of the woodwork, it takes us back in a sense to this ancient palace of Persia. Esther has to face the phobia and the craziness of a Haman who fears for his manliness and for his wholeness. Assuerus is really any old monarch, since throughout history rulers have shown themselves capable both of shielding Jews and of wiping them out. He can choose to give them a place in his realm, or else save his realm by eradicating them. It all hangs on his ability to overcome his castration anxiety, to listen to the voice of the feminine spoken by a matron or by a queen, or else heard only by his inner ear.

It all points towards our next investigation, arising from an awkward question:

Is anti-Semitism a problem of virility? Could the hatred of Jews really be to some extent a war between the sexes?

CHAPTER THREE

Anti-Semitism and the War of the Sexes

The philosopher Jacques Derrida once took out his copy of the famous essay written by Jean-Paul Sartre at the end of the Second World War, *Anti-Semite and Jew*, and came across this sentence:

> The Jew is [a man] whom other men consider a Jew: that is the simple truth from which we must start.[13]

However, in the copy he was reading, there was a misprint. An extra letter in the French expression for "a man" turned this naturally masculine word into a feminine noun: *une homme*.[14] That is where we could start from: a spelling mistake that allows us to surmise that at many points in history, Jews were seen as men of feminine gender, or at any rate as being marked as feminine in their action on the world.

13 Jean-Paul Sartre, *Anti-Semite and Jew* [1946], trans. George Becker (New York: Schocken, 1948), p. 49.
14 Quoted in *Judéités: questions pour Jacques Derrida*, ed. Joseph Cohen and Raphael Zagury-Orly (Paris: Galilée, 2003), p. 27.

In 2015, Roland Dumas, a veteran politician who had served as chair of one of France's most important constitutional bodies, said that he thought that the prime minister, Manuel Valls, was "under influence" because he was married to a Jewish woman. It's an ancient anti-Semitic trope: Jewish temptresses seduce men in power all the better to manipulate them and then "Jewify" them like velvet-gloved gaolers. The legend makes it obvious where a man's weakness comes from—it comes from the Jewish woman behind him, or inside him; and so Jews' relationship to political power forever remains beholden in some measure to a feminine plot.

In the 1930s, a French socialist who was a Jew became prime minister. One journalist described Léon Blum as "a bluestocking who sparkles in salon society and stuns it. Watch him at a rally: he's the female circling the male, sniffing it, making up to it—or else threatening it with wailing." Right-winger Léon Daudet called him "the girlie" and "the little miss" because he had "female tantrums and palpitations". For Charles Maurras, Léon Blum was "Blumah Bloom, baptised with secateurs"; the right-wing paper *Action française* described him as "a hysterical woman" and the Communist daily *Humanité* called him a "society hostess".[15]

15 The sources for all these references can be found in Pierre Birnbaum, *Léon Blum: Prime Minister, Socialist, Zionist* (New Haven: Yale University Press, 2015).

The feminisation of Jews in political discourse tends to make weaklings of Jewified men, or to present Jews as manipulators, hysterics or opportunists. All these motifs come from the traditional rhetoric of misogyny, and their purpose is to disqualify individuals from the exercise of power.

Jewish menstruation

The feminisation of Jews isn't only about their characters. Many anti-Semitic writings argue that it is not just the minds of Jews but also their bodies that are deficient in virility. Since the Middle Ages, anti-Jewish polemics have claimed that Jews bleed every month through one or another of their orifices, principally the nose and the anus. The theme of the haemorrhoidal Jew recurs frequently in depictions of Jews and in stories about them (giving rise to many Jewish jokes about piles).

In the thirteenth century, a famous Christian anatomist, Thomas of Cantimpré (1201–1272), claimed that Jewish males menstruated, which was taken as proof of an ancestral curse: the bleeding was taken to be the penalty paid for spilling the blood of Jesus. The logic is clear: because they caused blood to be shed, they must bleed themselves . . . and that leaves us free to bleed them dry.

The blood theme is also at the root of the accusations of ritual murder. Jews were supposed to sacrifice Christian children in an attempt to obtain their own salvation, or else to replenish the blood lost in menstruation.[16] Traces of fantasies of this kind can be found as late as the seventeenth century.

At the end of the nineteenth century, a whole new school and "science" of the Jewish race arose which went on to provide the main basis for Nazi ideology. Works of this genre systematically treat the Jewish body as biologically distinct. Research in this field was pursued well into the twentieth century and often provided support for the idea that Jewish virility was unnatural.

The case of Otto Weininger

In mind and body, Jewish men are women: that was the claim made by "scientific" researchers who listed the features they had in common, such as hysteria, instability, manipulativeness or even a liking for money.

Hitler's polemical writings were largely based on these ideas, taken principally from the works of Otto Weininger,

16 Sander Gilman, *The Case of Sigmund Freud: Medicine and Identity at the Fin de Siècle* (Baltimore: Johns Hopkins University Press, 1993), pp. 97–8, gives further examples of anti-Semitic legends about Jewish menstruation.

whom Hitler would later declare to be "the only honest Jew who exists".

Weininger, who nursed deep hatred for his own Jewish origins, published *Geschlecht und Charakter* ("Sex and Character") in 1903, when he was only twenty-three. Shortly after, he committed suicide, killing the Jew that was in himself.

Sex and Character was a bestseller in the early years of the twentieth century.[17] Here are two key passages:

> If one thinks about Woman and the Jew one will always be surprised to realise the extent to which Judaism in particular seems to be steeped in femininity, the nature of which I have so far only tried to explore in contrast to masculinity. [p. 276]

> Our age is not only the most Jewish, but also the most effeminate of all ages. [p. 299]

Whatever did Weininger mean by this? In his detailed listing of all the features he claims to be shared by women and Jews, the central element common to the two identities is "the duplicity that basically constitutes Judaism" (p. 294)

17   Otto Weininger, *Sex and Character: An Investigation of Fundamental Principles* [1906], trans. Ladislaus Löb, ed. Laura Marcus (Bloomington: Indiana University Press, 2005).

and which he claims to be at the root of the crisis of European society at that time.

In Weininger's view, Jews are the incarnation of ambiguity and of the fundamental inner duality that is a threat to every individual. Jews represent the Other that contaminates the Same, the flaw in the self that one seeks to overcome. That is why Jews destroy the world by introducing both doubt and duality—and Weininger plays on the common syllables in the German words *zwei* ("two") and *Zweifel* ("doubt") to assert that the Jewish mind is the "reign of two" that stands in the way of "making One".[18]

That is why Weininger sees Jewish culture as the opposite of Christian values and contrary to Aryan identity. The latter both aspire to wholeness and have no place for doubt. Aryan identity in particular treasures unity above all else: one people, one empire, one supreme leader.

What Weininger proposes is nothing less than a "path to redemption". In his mind, controlling women and Jews is to banish them from the self and to be free of them. The vital task is to get rid of the other that prevents us from being ourselves, so as to be at last "at one" with the self. Weininger's book is obsessed with cleansing the self of the Jew within. In his eyes, "Jewish sexuality" is the

18 Christina von Braun, "Le 'juif' et la 'femme': deux stéréotypes de l'autre dans l'antisémitisme allemand du XIXe siècle", *Revue germanique internationale* 5 (1996), pp. 123–39.

embodiment of the moral depravity that the Jewish body creates.

"The Jew is always more lecherous, more lustful, than the Aryan man," according to Weininger (p. 281). Like women, Jews are more subject to the pleasures of the senses and of the flesh. Weininger scoured the pseudosciences of *fin de siècle* Europe which associated Jewishness with sexual obsessions and crimes of passion. Jack the Ripper was often said to be Jewish, and this identity was frequently stressed as a key to understanding his homicidal mania. As Otto Rank pointed out in 1905, "other so-called anti-Semitic researchers claim that the sexual component plays a larger physiological role in Jews, as in all parasites, than in other 'species' or races."[19]

The sexual theme in anti-Jewish writing was already present in antiquity: Tacitus, for example, called Jews *projectissima ad libidinem gens*, "the most libidinous people on earth", with the laxest moral standards. There's nothing very new under the sun, except a dash of *fin de siècle* pseudoscience reviving an ancient obsession.

19 Otto Rank, "The Essence of Judaism", quoted in Gilman, *The Case of Sigmund Freud*, p. 26.

The childhood of a leader

In 1939, Jean-Paul Sartre published *The Childhood of a Leader*, a short story describing the upbringing, experience and intellectual development of Lucien Fleurier, a young man from a privileged background who turns into a militant anti-Semite. The story analyses the underpinnings of authoritarianism by means of a *Bildungsroman*, and shows how hatred becomes the bulwark of Fleurier's identity. Sartre enquires into what can lead a sensitive boy and an adventure-seeking adolescent to such a deadly outcome.

The beginning and the end of the tale set alongside each other provide us with a subtle key to understanding.

The story begins with an initiation, in the form of a significant memory from the hero's earliest years. On some religious feast day, a family friend, holding the infant in his arms and assuming he is a little girl, teases him:

> "What's your name? Jacqueline? Lucienne? Margot?"
> Lucien turned red and said, "My name is Lucien."
> He was no longer quite sure about not being a little girl . . . He was afraid that people might suddenly decide he wasn't a little boy any more.[20]

20 Jean-Paul Sartre, *Intimacy and Other Stories*, trans. Lloyd Alexander (London: Spearman, 1948), p. 135.

Sartre starts the story with gender confusion—the child's anxiety about his own sex—as if it constituted the developmental foundation of the authoritarian personality. He ends it with the hero's metamorphosis, where Lucien identifies himself entirely as an anti-Semite, the detestation of Jews having become the sole pillar of his own identity.

I am Lucien! Someone who can't stand Jews! [p. 230]

And this is how Sartre describes his hero's sense of identity:

Lucien's anti-Semitism was of a different sort: unrelenting and pure, it stuck out of him like a steel blade menacing other breasts. "It's . . . sacred," he thought. [p. 231]

In this sacred transformation, which resembles some religious ceremony of anti-Semitic confirmation, Lucien takes two decisions. First, one day he will marry a virgin:

He would marry her, she would be *his* wife, the tenderest of his rights . . . [and] he would tell her: "You belong to me!" What she would show him she would have the right to show to him alone, and for him the act of love would be a voluptuous counting of his goods. His most tender right, his most intimate right: the right to be respected to the very flesh, obeyed to the very bed. [p. 234]

In the wake of this resolution, Lucien makes a second decision: to grow a moustache! *The Childhood of a Leader* is a story that makes the search for manliness, or, more precisely, the threat to its hero's virility, the mainspring of the turn to authoritarianism and anti-Semitism. A young man who doubts his sexual identity and masculine integrity learns to protect his vulnerability beneath a majestic and reassuring hatred, and in the total control of a submissive female. That is what makes him a man, a male and also, undoubtedly . . . "a leader among Frenchmen".

A disease of men?

Could it be that in central Europe at the end of the nineteenth century men suffered from a crisis of virility? That's what Élisabeth Badinter suggests in *XY: On Masculine Identity*, where she also points out that an anxiety over identity that many scholars have described[21] was "not unre-

21 See Jacques Le Rider, *Modernity and Crises of Identity: Culture and Society in Fin-de-Siècle Vienna*, trans. Rosemary Morris (Cambridge: Polity, 1993).

lated to the rise of Nazism and more generally to European Fascism. Hitler's accession to power resonated unconsciously with the promise that manliness would be restored."[22] The turn of the twentieth century witnessed an outbreak of misogynistic works and denigrations of women at a time when calls for the political emancipation of women were growing ever louder. What worried Viennese intellectuals, Badinter writes, "was not so much the dissolution of the traditional family unit . . . as the emancipation of the middle-class woman".[23]

In the same years, the publishing of anti-Semitic literature reached an all-time peak. In it, Jews figured as "less than" men and as feminised males. Jewish women, on the other hand, are frequently presented as emancipated viragos, that is to say, as virile women. These two complementary anti-Semitic stereotypes of the masculine woman and the feminine man embody a threat to masculine domination and the gender norms of the society of the time.

Other writers establish a more or less direct connection between hatred of Jews and the crisis of masculinity. Theodor Adorno's contribution to *The Authoritarian Personality* (1950), for example, explored the link between anti-Semitism and the authoritarian personality grounded

22 Élisabeth Badinter, *XY: On Masculine Identity*, trans. Lydia Davis (New York: Columbia University Press, 1995), p. 17.
23 Badinter, *XY*, p. 15.

in patriarchy and a propensity to prejudice. Shulamit Volkov, for her part, showed that early-twentieth-century anti-Semitism was a "cultural code" linking people opposed to ideas of emancipation, particularly of women.[24] And Margarete Mitscherlich, pursuing Adorno's ideas about "the authoritarian personality", maintained that anti-Semitism is a "masculine malady".[25] Hatred of Jews, in her account, is a "pathology of the superego" and a means of projection of repressed desires onto Jews so as to be rid of the desires, and of Jews. As this phenomenon is directly connected to castration anxiety, it affects men more than women, and is evidence of the patriarchal structure of modern society. Women may of course also be affected, but for that to happen they must adopt and promote patriarchal stereotypes for themselves.

The image of the Jew as an unmanly man threatening the physical and psychological integrity of the male and therefore the integrity of the nation or the group looms large behind the tidal wave of twentieth-century anti-Semitism.

24 Shulamit Volkov, *Antisemitismus als kultureller Code* (Munich: Beck, 2000).
25 Margarete Mitscherlich-Nielsen, "Antisemitismus—eine Männerkrankheit?", in Günther Bernd Ginzel, ed., *Antisemitismus: Erscheinungsformen der Judenfeindschaft gestern und heute* (Cologne: Wissenschaft und Politik, 1991), pp. 337–42.

The "little Jew" and the "big goy"

What if there was a grain of truth in anti-Semitic slurs about Jews lacking manliness? American scholar Daniel Boyarin dared ask this provocative question in *Unheroic Conduct: The Rise of Heterosexuality and the Invention of the Jewish Man*. What if there were "something correct—although seriously misvalued—in the persistent European representation of the Jewish man as a sort of woman?"[26]

In the Talmud and in many rabbinical legends, we find the world of the Romans and the world of the Jews set against each other as two different kinds of masculinity.

Several stories present this archetypal opposition as a conflict of genders. The best known and most emblematic of these confrontations sets Reish Lakish against Rabbi Yohanan.

Reish Lakish was a marauder from Tiberias in the third century CE. A famously strong man, he became a gladiator, according to legend, adopting a way of life far removed from rabbinical ideals. One day his path crossed that of Rabbi Yohanan, a wise man celebrated in the Talmud not only for his great learning but also for his handsome looks and for not having any facial hair. He was the opposite

26 Daniel Boyarin, *Unheroic Conduct: The Rise of Heterosexuality and the Invention of the Jewish Man* (Berkeley: University of California Press, 1997), p. 3.

of an alpha male. He had a woman's face. This is what happened when they met:

One day, Rabbi Yoḥanan was bathing in the Jordan River. Reish Lakish saw him and jumped into the Jordan, pursuing him ... Rabbi Yoḥanan said to Reish Lakish: Your strength is fit for Torah study. Reish Lakish said to him: Your beauty is fit for women. Rabbi Yoḥanan said to him: If you return to the pursuit of Torah, I will give you my sister in marriage, who is more beautiful than I am. Reish Lakish accepted upon himself to study Torah. Subsequently, Reish Lakish wanted to jump back out of the river to bring back his clothes, but he was unable to return, as he had lost his physical strength. [Babylonian Talmud, Bava Metzia 84a]

A strange encounter of two worlds by the riverbank: Reish Lakish is deceived by the sight of a hairless body swimming in the water. He thinks he's seen a woman, jumps in to catch her up, probably intending rape. But the woman is in fact a sage with no expertise in physical violence, but well prepared for verbal jousting. That's how he persuaded the gladiator to swim to "the other side", to leave the masculine world of Rome and to come over to the rabbis' side. But as soon as he accepts, he loses the physical strength to swim on. Reish Lakish has swapped his muscles for a different kind of strength, the force of mind and words. It's not a castration in any sense: in the deal, Reish Lakish even gains a woman, Rabbi Yoḥanan's sister. But he now has a different kind of masculinity.

Boyarin thinks this other way of being a man was devised by rabbis in the first centuries of the Common Era, presumably as a reaction against the dominant mode of masculinity of the era. It functioned as retrospective appropriation of the physical and political impotence that Rome conventionally ascribed to Jews. In the end, the rabbis adopted the same view and claimed it as their own, transforming it from a handicap into a strength; by defining themselves "against" a non-Jewish archetype, they turned it into a negative model. That is what drove them to value non-muscular masculinity as a counterpart to the virility of gladiators and legionnaires; in so doing they also firmed up their own physical stereotype of the non-Jew. "Jews needed a model to define themselves against," says Boyarin, "and so they came up with the figure of the 'goy' as a hyperbolic inversion of their own norms." This conflict of two types of masculinity is not unrelated to the custom of circumcision. The Romans were horrified by it and saw it as a kind of castration.

By this argument, the atypical gender of Jewish males provided a tool of resilience, a way of turning what could have been a handicap into a means for the construction of identity. Jews got subtlety, cunning and a gift for words . . . and goys got muscles, vulgarity and weaponry skills. This literary caricature of non-Jews thus allowed a historically weak people to rebuild its honour and dignity.

You can find traces of this development in common metaphors and turns of phrase in various languages. In Yiddish, the thumb, which is the largest of the fingers and the one that permits the hand's grasp, is sometimes called "the goy". In French, there's an anti-Semitic way of talking about the sensation you get when you hit the funny bone in your elbow. Since the tingle goes right down the arm and into your little finger, it's called *le coup du petit juif*, "the little Jew's trick".

Wo/men

Did Jews accept the feminisation solely as a way of coping with domination? Was it just resilience, or did it exist prior to the conflict with Rome?

Readers of the Bible can get a glimpse of it in the books of the Prophets, where Hosea, Isaiah and many others are strangely keen on the same allegory, presenting the relationship between Jews and their God as if it were a marriage. It's a love story, where the knot is tied on Mount

Sinai and then put to the test. Like any love relationship, it has its high and low points, reconciliations and marital crises. The people are described at different times as faithful, rebellious, submissive and adulterous. But always, the people are given a feminine gender in relation to a male God. This amorous allegory is represented in the most famous of the Bible's lyrical texts, the Song of Songs, where the shepherd and the shepherdess personify the relationship between Israel and the God of Israel. In each of the books of the Prophets, the Jewish people take on the features of a woman in a relationship with a transcendent male.

The Bible certainly also contains personifications of masculine strength such as Samson and Joshua, alongside powerful warriors and great priests with perfect bodies. But the rabbis never choose these men as models of Jewish identity.

The rabbis' favourite heroes, the ones they praise in daily prayers, are characters of a different kind—partly vulnerable, and often with a handicap. They are not models of physical strength, and they are never invincible.

Abraham suffers from sterility, a considerable handicap in a patriarchal society that views offspring as a sign of divine blessing. Isaac is said to be blind, weak and easily swayed. Jacob is a frightened weakling with a limp. As for Moses, he has a stammer.

In short, none of these great figures is a model of hyper-virility or muscular masculinity, but each of them shows the ability to overcome a handicap and to be resilient. These heroes are not women, but they have something in common with the role of women in the Scriptures: a kind of assumed incompleteness, a specific impotence that is the paradoxical source of their legitimacy and their ability to act. They base their leadership on their weaknesses, as if their strength came from a disability overcome, from a "less than" which they turn into a "more than".

Jewish ritual constantly keeps this idea going and renews its foundations on this fracture, restaging it in a thousand and one ways. It starts with the ritual of circumcision. When a boy child enters the community on the eighth day of his life and has his foreskin removed in the traditional manner, prayers are said at the moment the skin is cut. The verses, of great antiquity, come from the book of Hosea, but, in a peculiar inversion of genders, they are all spoken as if addressed to a woman, since Hebrew is a language that marks the gender of the person spoken to.

This oddity has prompted some scholars to say that the circumcision ritual inscribes the feminine in the body of the newborn male.[27] In Hebrew, what is hollow or oblit-erated is called *nekeva*, which also means feminine. From

27   Daniel Boyarin, "'This We Know to Be the Carnal Israel': Circumcision and the Erotic Life of God and Israel", *Critical Inquiry* 18:3 (1992), pp. 474–505.

this point on, the boy child has in himself a void that creates through its absence the necessary condition for a relationship with the transcendent. Judaism does not claim that only Jews have access to this relationship, but it does suggest that this is how they turn their awareness into ritual and so do not fail to pass it on.

For the rabbis, circumcision was not a kind of castration: on the contrary, true Jewish masculinity arises from this rite of passage, as if the severing of the foreskin "phallicised" the Jewish male. Through its rejection of a body part, circumcision creates the necessary condition for a relationship to something greater than the self. Lack gives rise to a search for something other than the self, the quest for a severed-from-self with which you will never be One.

Self-construction over an abyss

Rabbinical Judaism proposes something strange: to ground your identity on an act of severance, on a "less than" which establishes belonging.

Its ability to formulate this idea to the point of making it the cornerstone of an immaterial edifice may well simply come from the fact that it was itself historically constructed on an absence of no small magnitude: that of the Temple of Jerusalem.

Jewish rabbinical thought is post-traumatic, and flourished most extensively in the time of that fundamental mourning. The hegemony of priestly Judaism came to an end in 70 CE with the collapse of the geographical centre point of the faith. A "theological" approach to the catastrophe was needed. How could you explain the fact that a God had allowed his residence to be torn down? Divine "omnipresence" in the world would not explain why he had let his house be destroyed and his city be ruined.

From then on rabbinical thinking, and particularly its mystical branch, adopted the idea of the "withdrawal" of the divine as a presence of the absence that underpins its faith.

The genius of the rabbis was to build on the abyss, and to offer resilience to an entire people by showing that it could rebuild its identity on the break-up of the world of the past.

That is the sense in which Judaism is the product of a fracture, the residue of a collapse. It stands above an abyss that does not seek to be filled in. It transforms what could have destroyed it into a regenerative force, a force that is present in all Jewish rituals. It is there in the formal conclusion of every marriage ceremony, when a glass has to be smashed. That is not only a way of harking back to the destruction of a temple almost two thousand years ago, but a way of reminding every new household and every construction to come that *Jewish life is built on the awareness of an incompleteness that stands in lieu of a foundation.* The desire to exist comes from the absence of being, as does desire itself, which ensures the future.

As Sigmund Freud pointed out long after the rabbis, "Only after the collapse of the visible Temple did the invisible edifice of Judaism become possible."[28]

In that sense, Judaism is a peculiar challenge: its invisible edifice prompted a whole people to move on and to exist elsewhere, not so as to repair or rebuild any visible monument, but so as to rise above the abyss.

Jewish identity is always built on ruins and on the awareness that it has something to do with a breach between the self and the self. Jacques Derrida put it this way: "The more you break up self-identity, the more you are saying 'My self-identity consists in not being identical to myself, in being foreign, the non-self-coinciding one,' etc., the more you are Jewish!"[29]

Why, then, if Judaism grounds identity in absence and invisible dislocation, does that make it especially deserving of hatred? What have the "theology of the void" and the

28 Letter to Martha Bernays, July 23, 1882, in Ernst Freud, ed., *The Letters of Sigmund Freud*, trans. Tania and James Stern (New York: Basic Books, 1960), p. 19.
29 Jacques Derrida, *Questioning Judaism: Interviews by Elisabeth Weber*, trans. Rachel Bowlby (Stanford: Stanford University Press, 2004), p. 41.

spirituality of absence got to do with obsessive anti-Semitism?

The invisible edifice Freud speaks of is paradoxically what has allowed Judaism to persist. Jewish self-construction on the fragmentary has created a system that is almost shatterproof. And that is the main reproach that anti-Semites have never stopped harping on over the centuries: the sheer lasting power of Jews.

Building on the broken is probably one of the keys to the persistence of Judaism. What's missing is indestructible for as long as it does not get replaced, but it constantly arouses the all too human temptation to be rid of it. What anti-Semites desperately try to be rid of is just such an identity gap. Daniel Sibony, a psychoanalyst, sees the fracture inside Jewish identity (or the fracture projected onto Jews) lying at the heart of the "enigma of anti-Semitism".

> People who refuse to recognise and take on board the reduplicated nature of their identities become or already are virtual anti-Semites . . . Hating Jews is in the first place to hate your own identity gap.[30]

Anti-Semites are easily persuaded that by getting rid of Jews they will instantly recover the wholeness to which they aspire. Hating Jews is a fantasy gap-filler.

30   Daniel Sibony, *L'Énigme antisémite* (Paris: Seuil, 2004), p. 90.

Fethi Benslama, a psychoanalyst who works with radicalised Muslim youngsters who are very receptive to anti-Semitic rhetoric, refers to the same obsession with an identity gap:

When radicalisation is on offer with its promise of a total ideal, a heroic mission for a sacred cause, these young people respond, they feel they are becoming powerful, their gaps are filled in, and they are ready to go to heaven.[31]

To have and have not

Anti-Jewish hatred rests on a paradoxical accusation.

At first sight anti-Semites appear always to blame Jews for having something that they do not. Jews "have" access— access to power, money, luck or the life to which the hater aspires. Jews appear to have taken something away from the rest of humanity, to have usurped some other persons' shares, to have prevented the nation or the group from being One. To enjoy something "as a Jew" is to deprive someone else of that thing.

At the same time, Jews are seen by some as being

31 Interviewed in *Les Inrocks*, May 15, 2016.

less-than-men. Jews "don't have" full manliness and they threaten the boundaries of the group by what is cut off. Jews are gaps, they are dirty, they are "holes" and they arouse anti-Semites' castration anxiety. They are reminders of identity gaps, of the absence of being, of everything that seems to prevent their enemies from being completely and entirely themselves.

That's the whole paradox. Anti-Semites believe they can blame Jews for HAVING something that they do not . . . but they also blame Jews for NOT HAVING something (which anti-Semites don't have either) and for getting on fine without it. Out, damned spot! Jews not only hark back to the impossibility of an identity without gaps, not only do they represent the void that anti-Semites would like to be rid of, but what's more, they survive, they manage, and even manage rather well by making that gap the foundation of their unending rebirth.

CHAPTER FOUR

Why Choose the Jews?

Let's move on to one of the biggest reasons for anti-Jewish hatred: their controversial status as the "chosen people". Fuelled by often wilful misapprehensions, anti-Semites frequently claim that the Jews' chosen-ness gives them a democratic justification for being angry. They wonder: just who are these people who think they are so special? Anti-Semites frequently allege that equality and justice support their opposition to the arrogant Jews who stand in the way of human harmony and the triumph of the universal.

Of course, they leave aside the fact that Judaism itself has never managed to give a precise definition of the chosen-ness that's been hung around its neck. Of course, they leave aside the fact that in the endless discussions of the term in the Scriptures not one of the sages interprets it as granting Jews essential superiority over others. Anti-Semites often know much better than Jews do what it means to be "the chosen people" and what it keeps from those who are not chosen.

Here is how the Hebrew word first comes up in the

Bible. God says he is forming a special kind of bond with the Hebrews that he calls a covenant. He establishes a specific relationship with the Israelites, whom he calls his "favourite children". An exclusive contract between a people and its god is not particularly unusual: there are many groups, tribes and clans who believe they have a special relationship with a divinity. Most of the foundation myths of ancient cultures contain a story about a contract with a divinity that provides exclusive protection to the original group.

However, through the mouths of the Prophets, the Old Testament hints that God has connections not only with Israel but also with other peoples.

> To Me, O Israelites, you are just like the Ethiopians— declares the LORD. True, I brought Israel up from the land of Egypt, but also the Philistines from Caphtor and the Arameans from Kir. [Amos 9:7]

This passage from the book of Amos has a drastic effect on the idea of an exclusive connection between God and the Hebrews. It is sung in synagogues whenever a particular part of Leviticus is read (a part that the sages associate with the reading of the prophecy of Amos), which deals with the separation of the Jews:

If you will obey me faithfully and keep my covenant, you shall be my treasured possession among all the peoples. Indeed, all the earth is Mine, but you shall be to me a kingdom of priests and a separate people. [Exodus 19:5–6][32]

To be blunt: when Jews in synagogue say "We are a holy nation", what they are reading at the same time says "Sure, but we're not the only ones!"

The particular relationship between God and the children of Israel is therefore not easy to analyse. What does their particular mission consist of? It has been variously interpreted as a duty, a task to undertake, and as a responsibility falling on them as a collectivity, without an obligation to convert the rest of the world to that mission. Sometimes it is defined as a testimony that this people should bear to the whole of humanity simply by being there. In the Torah, the "chosen-ness" of the Jewish people is never defined as natural superiority.

---

32 Translator's note: "A separate people" translates the Hebrew *kadosh*, from the verb *lekadesh*, "to distinguish" or "to separate". Although translations of this verse from Exodus usually give the sense of "holy" to *kadosh* (the King James Bible has "a kingdom of priests, and an holy nation", for example), Mme Horvilleur restores what she takes to be the original meaning of a word that has several different potential translations.

Were the Jews picked, or lumbered?

The Hebrew term *am segoula* is translated into English as "chosen people" and in French as "the elected people" (*peuple élu*), but neither version represents the original meaning very well. The sense of it could be expressed as "treasure people", "medicine people", or even as "distinct people" or "people capable of making distinctions". As written Hebrew words typically have several meanings, these translations are all possible, but none is completely explicit. In what way could a people be a precious medicine or a cure? What is it supposed to heal, or to distinguish? And especially, in what way could such an attribute constitute a privilege?

Jews take the trouble to wonder what it means to be chosen, but oddly enough, anti-Semites are not so uncertain. They appear to take Jewish Scripture far more literally than Jews do themselves. Given their history, Jews are more likely to say: "If our being chosen really does give us a place in the sun, then it could hardly have been kept under wraps for so long!" No matter: others do believe in it, come what may, and reproach Jews for their exclusive, and excluding, superiority.

There's a well-known story about two Jews sitting side by side on a bench reading newspapers. One of them suddenly realises that his partner is reading an anti-Semitic rag.

"How can you read such rubbish?" he asks.

"Because it really cheers me up," his neighbour answers. "It says we have power and money and run the world. Now wouldn't that be nice?"

The idea of the Jews being chosen often serves to support the image of the arrogant, over-confident Jew. Whatever their place in society and however vulnerable they may be, Jews bear the privilege they are assumed to have, or that people believe their holy book grants them.

In the last analysis, the problem of the Jews being chosen isn't really a Jewish problem at all. In 1938, Sigmund Freud wrote in *Moses and Monotheism*:

> I venture to assert that the jealousy which the Jews evoked in the other peoples by maintaining that they were the first-born, favourite child of God the Father has not yet been overcome by those others, just as if the latter had given credence to the assumption.[33]

For the founder of psychoanalysis, the problem was not to find out what Jews believed, but to understand why some non-Jews give such credit to those claims.

The metaphor of the family used by Freud in this passage is not at all random. What seems to be at stake in

33 Sigmund Freud, *Moses and Monotheism*, trans. Katharine Jones (New York: Knopf, 1939), p. 147.

the issue of the Jews' "chosen-ness" is a relationship to origins and the problem of a child's status within the monotheist family. The first-born may shrug it all off and say: "I do not know what the closeness of God and his confidence in me expressed in this passage really means, but I can assure you that it is really not important." But the question remains an open one for those who come after and also claim the inheritance of the original revelation. They assert their succession to a message that had been delivered before, but to someone else.

The choosing of the first-born may then come to seem like a privilege of birth—the right of primogeniture. It challenges the next-born to ask: is there enough room for me in the arms of the divine?

Junior siblings have various ways of making themselves as "chosen" as their elders, or of enjoying an equally intense relationship with the transcendent. They can say God may make more than one covenant, just as a parent may love more than one child; or they can say that the original relationship has been superseded. As in any band of brothers, the youngest can be blessed like none before him; alternatively, junior siblings may claim that their elders have betrayed or abused their inheritance (sadly, this approach seems to have been the more popular in the course of human history). The issues of chosen-ness and primogeniture are intrinsically connected, since both deal with sibling rivalry and family background. They constantly arise in inter-faith conflicts of every era, and they are intolerable to fundamentalists of every tradition. What makes a fundamentalist, after all, is the claim that his tradition comes direct from its source and is untainted by any other: naturally, fundamentalists can't accept that some other tradition heard the message first and handed it on.

Chosen-ness also raises the central question of Revelation. What did the first person hear, and why was he the only person invited to hear it? Judaism does not seek to make converts because, unlike Christianity and Islam, it does not claim to have a universal mission. This has given rise to a suspicion that Jews intercepted the message they heard in the desert and kept it for themselves. Why don't they want to broadcast the good word to the whole world?

The doorstep salesman story

So why did God choose the Jews? Many rabbinical legends try to answer the question, and some of them even turn it into a joke.

One such legend says that before God gave the Torah to the Jews he knocked on lots of doors offering other nations a covenant with him, and the Torah too. But there were no buyers: all shut the door on him, until at last he found the Jews (Midrash Pesikta Rabbati). Those rabbis had the wit and the cheek to see their God as an old-fashioned door-step salesman trying to unload his Scripture as if it were an encyclopaedia that nobody really needs. That's a long way from traditional images of piety!

Another Talmudic legend has it that the Hebrews were no keener on the covenant than other peoples, but at the moment of Revelation, God raised Mount Sinai over them like a lid, and said: "Either you accept the Torah, or I'll drop the mountain on you and that will be the end of you." Commenting on Exodus 19:17—"and they took their places at the foot of the mountain"—Rabbi Avdimi bar Ḥama bar Ḥasa said:

the Jewish people actually stood beneath the mountain, and the verse teaches that the Holy One, Blessed
be He, overturned the mountain above the Jews
like a tub, and said to them: If you accept the Torah,
excellent, and if not, there will be your burial.
[Babylonian Talmud, Shabbat 88a]

That was a deal they couldn't refuse!

Over the ages, many poets have spun variations on the theme of a people who asked for nothing but had Revelation shoved down its throat like a pill it could have done without. The Israeli poet Yehuda Amichai (1924–2000), for example, put it this way:

> When God packed up and left the country, He left the Torah with the Jews. They have been looking for him ever since, shouting, "Hey, you forgot something, you forgot," and other people think shouting is the prayer of the Jews.[34]

A chosen people that never stops telling itself it could have done without the privilege is a far cry from the arrogance and condescension imputed to Jews by anti-Semites. Jews have never hesitated to say that whatever it is they were given was not gladly received.

But we still haven't identified what they were given. On that issue too, there are legends that say different things.

According to tradition, Revelation occurred in some indeterminate place in a desert lying between Egypt and the Promised Land. In Hebrew, the moment of revelation is called *hitgalut*, a word whose root, *galut*, also means exile. God thus revealed himself at Mount Sinai in an extraterritorial space, at a place that belongs to nobody and that no-one can pinpoint on a map, and where the people are

34 Yehuda Amichai, "Gods Change, Prayers are Here to Stay", in *Open Closed Open: Poems*, trans. Chana Bloch and Chana Kronfeld (New York: Harcourt, 2000), p. 40.

all on their way to somewhere else. God did not show himself in any people's or person's comfort zone, according to the rabbis, so that nobody may say it happened at *our* place, or that God spoke in *my* house.

All the Hebrews of the time—a whole generation of emancipated slaves—gathered at the foot of the mountain, but according to tradition they were not alone. It is said that not only were the living present at Sinai, but also the absent: the vanished generations and the generations to come, souls departed and yet to be born, were all at the rendezvous. The entire intergenerational community of the Hebrews aspired to hear and receive the Law.

But then things get rather murky. The Scriptures that deal with this central event, at the very heart of Jewish thought, are as clear as mud. They contain no official version and no clear exposition of what was given or revealed on that day in the desert. The huge mass of writing on the Revelation does not tell us exactly what was in it, leaving the full scope of what was heard by the Hebrews in permanent suspension.

There are many theories. Did the Hebrews receive the written Torah in the form in which it continues to be read, passed on and studied, as a set of scrolls to be kept safe in synagogues? The sages say no: a spoken Torah was revealed at the same time as the written Torah, with exegesis arising at the same time as the text (or even before it, according to some authorities), which made the Hebrews not so much the people of the book as the people of the interpreters of the book, in the words of Armand Abécassis. In this tradition, the Hebrews are said to have received at Revelation not only a written Law but also, by a bizarre phenomenon outside of historical time, the full set of commentaries that would later be made on the written Law. According to this legend, everything that would be explained by a sage to his teacher over the following centuries was revealed to Moses already at Mount Sinai.

You could call this the maximalist reading of Revelation. Everything that is to be said some day is already present in the founding moment, like a seed.

Other scholars take a more modest line. Not everything was revealed at Sinai, they say, and the people heard only what are called the Ten Commandments, or the Decalogue, which lay out a biblical ethical code in ten points as the foundation or prop of Revelation in its entirety. *I am the Lord thy God . . . thou shalt not kill . . . thou shalt not steal . . .*

By no means! other scholars respond in this unending argument. All we heard at Mount Sinai were the first two out of the ten commandments . . . But others say that what reached us was only the very first: *I am the Lord thy God which have brought thee out of the land of Egypt, out of the house of bondage.* They think that the Revelation at Mount Sinai was first and foremost a statement of the Hebrews' freedom and the recognition of a God that had freed them.

But that's not quite right either, according to other interpreters of Jewish tradition. The Hebrews gathered at the foot of the mountain, they claim, heard only one word. Just one. The first word of the first sentence of the first of the Ten Commandments: *anokh'i*, "I am". That, they say, is the secret: in place of a written Torah, an oral Torah, or a list of moral commands, Revelation was a divine "I" sounding across the desert that was heard by a whole people.

On the other hand, Kabbalists object, the people at Mount Sinai might have heard only a single letter. Just one: the first letter of the first word of the first sentence of the first of the commandments in the Decalogue. The Hebrews gathered at the foot of the mountain, they claim, including the generations of the deceased and the not yet born, heard only one sound, and it is really key, because the first letter of the word *anokh'i* is the *aleph*. And *aleph* is . . . a silent letter![35]

So at Mount Sinai people gathered for the greatest revelation in all the history of the Jews and they heard: nothing. A silence. The greatest silence of all time, the silence that echoes around the world. A fine privilege for a chosen people, to have been the only ones invited to listen to . . . nothing!

All the same, says Gershom Scholem, another great master of Jewish mysticism, the *aleph* is not completely silent.

In Hebrew, the consonant *aleph* represents nothing more than the position taken by the larynx when a word begins with a vowel. Thus the *aleph* may be said to denote the source of all articulate sound . . . Rabbi Mendel transformed the revelation on Mount Sinai into a mystical revelation, pregnant with infinite meaning, but without specific meaning.[36]

Put this way, the Revelation at Mount Sinai was neither a sound nor a silence, but a potential sound, a word not

35 Rabbi Menahem Mendel of Rymanov (1745–1815) is the main source of this teaching.
36 Gershom Scholem, *On the Kabbalah and its Symbolism*, trans. Ralph Manheim (New York: Schocken, 1969), pp. 29–30.

yet articulated. Revelation was not a voice, but a potential voice, it was the movement of a larynx, the potential initiation of speech.

At Mount Sinai the Hebrews were witness to a capacity for speech, which was not the autonomy of language that the Greeks called *logos*, but a subtle negotiation between a revealed Law (heteronomy) and the autonomy of its interpretation: a balance between legality and freedom.

At this point, the maximalist and minimalist versions of Revelation converge. Both argue that, at the beginning, in an indeterminate place that belongs to no-one where all the generations can be gathered together and united, an indeterminate gift was made to the Hebrews: the seed of all that could ever be said. The starting point was the revelation of the infinite potential of language and interpretation, of the residue of speech. The unsaid thus returns to Mount Sinai all who adhere to the continuity of the word, who know that the word comes from him, from an Other who is far greater than they can be.

Hedgehogs and foxes

In short, Revelation says that "everything" has not been said. That lies at the root of the chosen status of the Jews and of the hatred it arouses.

People have never stopped asking Jews: why do you keep the Word to yourselves? Why have you not wished to share it? Why were you the first to receive it and to do so like miserly Jews, on your own?

The most mystical and the most secular of Jews have replied in the same way, but with equally little effect: "We can assure you that we heard nothing—we just got a silent *aleph*!" That answer doesn't make the cut, because it leaves in suspense the question as to why it was only they and not everyone else that got the silent *aleph*. What obsesses anti-Semites is the "not everyone else".

> We can sum it up like this: the rites and customs of the Jews make it impossible to use the word *all* when we are talking about human beings. Whilst they live in the *oecumene* (the habitable world), they set themselves outside common humanity. For as long as they live on . . . they prevent us from speaking meaningfully of *all* human beings. They make it impossible to establish a complete and coherent picture of all human behaviour. Profane and sacred become ambiguous terms in themselves, and the difference between them becomes unclear. The only recourse to save the signifier *all* is to make an exception for Jews.[37]

37 Jean-Claude Milner, "Lacan le juif", *La cause freudienne* 79 (2011), pp. 68–9.

Many are the causes—empires, universal religions and humanist beliefs—that rely on the idea of a redemptive totality that is their Truth or their path to salvation. The Roman Empire, Christianity, Islam and the Enlightenment are all partly built on just such a dream of a universal account of everything, for everyone. Almost inevitably, however, at some point in their history they eventually stumble on what Milner calls "the noun Jew" as the name of the impossibility of completeness. To rescue their respective totalities, they often find themselves obliged to treat the bearer of the non-total as an exception.

Greek philosopher Archilochus is said to have said, "A fox knows many things, but a hedgehog one important thing." It seems that anti-Semitic hedgehogs can't abide a Jewish fox.

Jewish thinkers maintain they heard nothing but the infinite in the words of a god who told them: "Not everything has been said," but: "There is everything still to say." They claim that only a particular exception can save the dynamic of universalism from a totalitarian nightmare. They whisper to all and any who listen that Truth is never the "whole" Truth. Truth is either fragmented, or else it can lead to crimes.

Any universal ambition that does not pay attention to its own fractures and flaws, to the exceptions from which it is made, risks succumbing to the temptation of totalitarianism which, in order to save wholeness for everything, makes an exception of the Jews.

What is true of collective ambitions is equally applicable to the construction of the individual. Anti-Semites also seek to construct themselves or to rescue themselves by excluding Jews and by treating them as separate. This is how Jean-Paul Sartre described the phenomenon in his *Anti-Semite and Jew* in 1945:

> The anti-Semite is a man who is afraid. Not of the Jews, to be sure, but of himself, of his own conscious-ness, of his liberty, of his instincts, of his responsi-bilities, of solitariness, of change, of society, and of the world—of everything except the Jews . . . The anti-Semite is a man who wishes to be pitiless stone, a furious torrent, a devastating thunderbolt—any-thing except a man.[38]

Hatred of Jews is always constructed as a fear of every-thing and a dream of a totality that requires Jews to be excepted from it. "Except the Jews . . ." is what allows anti-Semites to be "safe and sound".

That is why the chosen-ness of the Jews will always excite the emotions of anti-Semites. It separates a group

38 Jean-Paul Sartre, *Anti-Semite and Jew* [1946], trans. George Becker (New York: Schocken, 1948), p. 38.

that anti-Semites have already chosen to set apart in order to define themselves. It provides textual support in the others' own Scripture for what anti-Semites have established as part of their own stories of identity.

CHAPTER FIVE

The Problem of Zionism

In a poll conducted by the European Commission in 2003 on a sample of 7,500 respondents throughout the European Union, Israel came out top in a strange contest. Respondents were asked to say whether or not each of fifteen countries listed "presents or not a threat to peace in the world".[39] Israel got a higher score than all others, including Iran, Iraq and North Korea. That tiny country was thus identified as the number-one obstacle to the concert of nations and the greatest risk to world peace. The result makes you wonder: is Israel seen as a threat for what it is, or for what it brings out in its neighbours? Is Israel a danger because it exists, or in virtue of what it provokes in its enemies?

This reminds us of Jean-Claude Milner's argument that we mentioned previously: the noun *Jew* (a name attached to Israel by many people today) refers to whatever prevents a group, or the world, from being *whole*, from being at

39 See *The Guardian*, November 1, 2003. The poll was never published, but leaked to the Spanish daily *El País*.

one in global peace. It's what stops us from making peace in the sense of the Hebrew word *shalom*, which literally means "plenitude" and "completeness". For the world to be at peace, it has to be rid of all that splits it apart, which is what Jews represent.

At various points in their histories, the Roman Empire, Christendom and Germany all came to that conclusion. The existence of the State of Israel appears to reactivate the same threat in a different manner, as it fractures the entente to which people aspire. What the survey respondents seemed to be saying was, "Ah, if only Israel weren't in the way . . ." then the world would be *whole* and full, or something like it. A part of the Arab world today appeals in a similar way to the loss of wholeness when it suggests that if Israel did not exist then the *ummah* would heal its divisions and live in calm.

Some people say that talking about Jews is not the same thing as talking about Israel. Agreed. However, the ineradicable confusion of the two words undoubtedly plays a central role in a conflict that has far more than its fair share of passionate engagement and media coverage.

Many Arab intellectuals are aware of this. Allegedly, Edward Said observed that the success of the Palestinian cause owed a lot to the identity of its opponents. The conflict would never have attracted so much attention, he said, if the Palestinians weren't fighting Jews.

Yuval Harari puts Jewish power in a humorous perspective and makes fun of the obsession of anti-Semitism:

> I would say to the anti-Semites: Get over it. Jews may be a very interesting people, but when you look at the big picture, you must realise that they have had a very limited impact on the world. Throughout history, humans have created hundreds of different religions and sects. A handful of them—Christianity, Islam, Hinduism, Confucianism and Buddhism—influenced billions of people . . . The central and most beautiful value of Judaism is modesty. We would do well to take this value to heart.[40]

Yet we have to admit that what is in international terms a micro-nation and a micro-land has played a disproportionate role in the passions and arguments of the modern world.

The question of Israel has become something of an obsession for some people, and it would be naive or else dishonest to claim this has nothing to do with the word *Jew* and all that this word has unleashed in the course of history. The word carries a symbolic weight far greater than what it refers to, which cannot be alien to the strength of the rejection it arouses.

40 Yuval Harari, "Judaism is Not a Major Player in the History of Humankind", *Haaretz*, July 31, 2016.

Over recent decades there has been a strange transformation in the use of words and in the images they suggest. In the wake of the Shoah, for instance, Jews were seen as a vulnerable and oppressed minority, and Israel was considered the legitimate refuge of a people that Europe had been unable or unwilling to rescue. A few decades later, Israel is viewed by many as a colonial regime based on military oppression that Europe permitted to exist out of a bad conscience. Jewish "Zionists" no longer attract much sympathy in Europe.

In the minds of many Europeans, Zionism, which was formerly a project for the emancipation and self-determination of Jews and the building of their national home, has now turned into a system for the colonial oppression and domination of the weak. This change underlies the arguments of all those who attack Israel less for its policies than for its existence.

The State of Israel has some responsibility for the change in the way it is seen. Its loss of sympathy is not unrelated to the political choices made by its leaders and the ultra-nationalist and messianic excesses of some of its politicians. Not unrelated, but perhaps also not in proportion.

What other nationalist and expansionist policies in the world are there that bring into question the legitimacy of the nation that carries them out?

Why do Israeli personalities, writers and artists who

visit European and American universities provoke demonstrations, whereas visiting speakers from Russia, China or Iran do not?

Whatever approach you take to the conflict, whether or not you make a distinction between anti-Semitism and anti-Zionism, whether or not you have a common understanding of what Zionism means,[41] you have to grant that some of the obsessive themes of anti-Israel sentiment hark back to the themes of traditional anti-Semitic discourse.

In the past Jews were accused of preventing the consolidation of the Empire, the nation or the people. They fractured their continuity and unity, and "contaminated" them with Jewish foreignness, the Jewish mind and Jewish beliefs.

Today Israel is accused of violating the continuity of an Arab world by being a foreign presence, a Western "implant" at the heart of Arab unity, which, as we all know, would do just fine if Israel weren't there ... As a result, Jews who claim to be Zionists are seen throughout the world as the accomplices of Arab fragmentation, with all the repercussions it may have on the rest of the world.

The accusations made against Zionists are often partial reflections of the historical experience of the accusers. In

41 The June 2018 issue of the French journal *Tenou'a*, edited by the author, features discussions of the different meanings of Zionism and of the variety of its contemporary interpretations.

France and in the UK, anti-Zionists see Israel as a colonial enterprise. In the United States, Israel is accused of being a racist state, and in South Africa, an echo of apartheid. Everywhere, anti-Zionist critique has an autobiographical slant.

As for the image of Jews in the Diaspora, that too has undergone a change, one that is not so much tied to Israel as to the postcolonial debate that has taken hold in Europe and elsewhere. With the growth of identity politics and competition for victim status, some people think that the memory of the Shoah takes up too much space. It's as if it has overshadowed other suffering and, absurd though this may seem, it has come to be an object of envy. What seems to be going on before our eyes is a morbid race for trauma, in which some tell the Jews: "You're not the only ones! What about the pain we suffered . . . and suffered before you?" Nowadays, there's nothing more precious or enviable than victim status, the privilege of a place in the shadow of some great misfortune that offers protection and standing as an oppressed group. It brings back to mind a phrase that Marceline Loridan-Ivens liked to quote: "They will never forgive us the harm they did to us."[42] Jewish suffering is both an archetype and an exception.

42 Marceline Loridan-Ivens (1928–2018) was a French film-maker who survived a year in Auschwitz, Bergen-Belsen and Theresienstadt in her teens.

Calls have been made in the name of past suffering—colonisation, discrimination and slavery—to fight whiteness, by which is meant the inheritance of the European dominant classes who did violence to the subaltern and who still remain privileged. It is a necessary and fundamental step to allow the voices to be heard of those others who were silenced for so long, provided it doesn't lead to the construction of an identity no less hate-filled and excluding than the one it challenges.

A controversial pamphlet appeared in France in 2016 that packed a great deal of resentment against the West into its few pages. Its author is the spokesman of the Parti des Indigènes de la République, the "Party of Natives in the Republic", which combats all forms of "imperial, colonial and Zionist domination".[43] Houria Bouteldja's *Whites, Jews and Us* argues that Whites are a "sociological" class that carries the fault of the West and is intrinsically guilty of colonial domination.[44]

Next to the Whites stand the Jews. They too have suffered, undeniably, but their pain does not entitle them to a place among the "racialised" subaltern. Why not? Because

43 *Indigènes*, "Natives", a term formerly used by French colonialists, is intended as a provocation.
44 Houria Bouteldja, *Les Blancs, les juifs et nous* (Paris: La Fabrique, 2016).

the Jews have been contaminated by the West and have become its accomplice. In a word, Jews have been "whitened". "You can't tell if someone is Jewish just because they say they are," she writes. "You can tell Jews by their hunger for being indistinguishable from Whites." Jews are "*dhimmis* in the French republic", or "Gurkhas of Western imperialism";[45] Zionism in this view is another form of White violence that has to be resisted by making anti-Zionism a "land of asylum" and the leading edge of the struggle against colonisation across the ages.

By some identitarian magic, all the excluded, the subaltern and the racialised have joined forces to become an "Us" against "Them", the guilty West. In this new fight by a decolonised totality, Jews are perceived as being at the cutting edge of all attempts to fragment it. Once again, they are the threat to *shalom*; they are the obstacle in the way of union, in Palestine as in the West. In Palestine, they are an obstacle because they support a colonial settlement that has become the alleged mother of all imperial adventures. In the West, they are an obstacle because they are alleged to be complicit in the oppressive values and philosophy of the Enlightenment's white universalism.

There's nothing very new under the sun! Once again,

---

45 A *dhimmi* is a non-Muslim enjoying protected but secondary status in traditional Muslim societies. Gurkhas are Nepalese soldiers who have traditionally fought in the British army.

Jews are the thorn in the side of historical wholeness and stand in the way of a great drive to unification. Everything has changed but everything stays the same. In the past, Jews prevented the dominant from saying "We". Today, they prevent the subaltern from forming a solid bloc. In the past they colonised minds, today they colonise land. It's always the Jews who stop the One by severing it or severing themselves from it.

But there is perhaps one real difference. The unity dreamed of by Bouteldja and that is threatened by Jewish particularism carries no imperial or national mission, nor is it the vehicle of a universal creed seeking to convert others. Quite the opposite, in fact: it is an expression of exacerbated "identitarianism", denouncing both the violence of universalism (apparently embodied by Diasporic Jews) and oppressive nationalism (represented by Israeli Jews).

We would be well advised to try to hear what contemporary identity politics is saying, and to listen to its denunciation of universalism and the values of the West.

Group identities have arisen left and right to deny individuals the right to speak in the first person singular. "No, my body does not belong to me," Bouteldja writes. "I now know that my place is among *my own folk*" (p. 95; our italics). Collective identity now trumps the Enlightenment value of individual emancipation: it's as if saying "I" turns you into a "White".

126

You can hear something of the same tune in some of the key struggles for individual emancipation, such as feminism. Nowadays, feminism sometimes has recourse to anti-universal arguments that turn the movement's origins on its head.

Some people now accuse universalist feminism of being a "white invention" and of seeking to emancipate women whether they like it or not, disconnecting them from the struggles they have to undertake on behalf of their "race" or religious community. In other words, they blame it for being a Western weapon that fragments identity: by seeking to free women, feminism allegedly severs them from a transcendent "We" and from keeping faith with something else.

Cultural appropriation

Identity politics is having a much wider impact in more fields than those we have mentioned. It is turning the polarities of "dominant/subaltern" and "coloniser/colonised" into a new criterion of value judgment with respect to groups and individuals. Jews are of course once again the site or the name of an exclusion in such a vision of the world.

Let's consider cultural appropriation. At the time of

writing, it seems to be mainly found in US academia, and in some universities it has become a favourite topic for heated argument. But by the time you read this translation, it's quite possible that the French will have coined a new word of their own for it. The question is: can any individual, but especially if they belong to the so-called dominant culture, adopt the dress codes, food styles and linguistic particularities of a different ethnic group, primarily of any group seen as historically subaltern? The argument goes like this: adopters could easily desecrate an item that is sacred to a culture that is not theirs if they popularise it outside of its original context. More seriously, they would in that way be repeating the violence done in the past by the dominant group to the subaltern that was robbed of its treasures. The issue is then to offer symbolic reparation for historical plunder by putting red lines around the culture of another group and not permitting any appropriation of what was originally part of that culture.

You can easily imagine the kind of disputes this idea can give rise to. Can I not wear a sombrero unless I am Mexican? May I sing gospel even if my ancestors weren't slaves? You may smile at such questions, but you should listen to the debates and try to understand what kind of "cultural revolution" they transmit to those who engage in them in the United States.

Sociologists Bradley Campbell and Jason Manning see arguments against cultural appropriation as manifestations of a "victimhood culture" that is replacing older "honour and dignity cultures". The latter type claims to uphold universal Western moral values and supports (sometimes naively) the right of individuals to be judged on their actions and not on their skin colour or ethnicity. But today some people are calling for a "victimhood culture" which makes skin colour and ethnicity part of the judgment made of an individual's actions. On this view, particular communities and groups, such as women or LGBT people, would deserve special treatment in light of their history and of past and present discrimination, whereas other individuals from groups identified as dominant or oppressive, notably heterosexual white males, would not.

It looks as though this class of historically privileged individuals is now required to make up for something. They are collectively tarred by a moral fault handed down over the generations by the group they identify with.

Such "victimhood culture" is certainly concerned with justice and reparation. It highlights the often unwitting transmission of the privileges that some classes and groups enjoy, and asks us to be vigilant. But it is also in contradiction with a universal principle of law: nobody may be accused of a crime they did not commit themselves. There can be no individual guilt for the collective crimes of anybody's ancestors, whether those ancestors are identified by ethnicity, colour, gender or anything else.

"We" is a misleading word

The culture war in the United States and the demands made by identity groups in Europe are both about atoning for collective guilt. Both involve reversing the two basic values of the Enlightenment, the dignity and autonomy of the individual.

It is extremely problematic to claim that individuals have specific rights or duties deriving from sufferings experienced or inflicted in the past by the group to which they belong. Does a black skin constitute the whole of Black experience through the ages? Does a white skin carry the burden of everything that people with similar pigmentation may have done in the past? You can say that these are intended as sociological, not biological categories. But what if a white person claims to be black? Who has the right to accept or deny such a claim?

In this identity-based view of the world, individuals are simply the history of their group. They are nothing more than the tribe they belong to. They can't say, "I am that and a thousand other things besides," or hint that they have nothing in common with their "communities". They have to be solid, and forget anything else that their own multiple identities might say about them, for fear of betraying their tribe.

All other inner voices are silenced: they are smothered by the narcissism of exclusivity that perpetually encloses people in their families and clans.

That is the ultimate paradox. A dominant system silenced the voices of minority groups over the centuries, but in order to correct that injustice, we are stifling minority voices that don't fit the fixed image that some people have of their group.

In attempting to right a wrong by illuminating some of the darkest corners of history and so giving minorities more visibility, we have established a system that negates the individual.

That is how the identitarian "we" is established. What is paradoxical about it is that it is used by individuals who claim the right to speak on behalf of a group. According to Jacques Derrida, "*We* is always uttered by one person . . . It's always a *me* that says *us*, an *I* that utters *we*."[46]

Identity speech when uttered by an individual always commits another, who may not assent to it, but is taken hostage by it whether he likes it or not. To put it another

46 Jacques Derrida, "Pour l'amour de Lacan", in *Résistances de la psychanalyse* (Paris: Galilée, 1996).

way, "we" is always a misleading expression. It attempts to make a Whole, sometimes at the cost of crushing anything that obstructs the consolidation of the group.

Joining hands

What has all this got to do with Jews or with Israel?

First, Jewish history amply demonstrates that attempts to make a Whole and to consolidate the group always end up stumbling over the Jews, or else rely on excluding them. As we have said before, Jews represent or revive the fracture that groups may think they can avoid.

Ideologies close to totalitarianism, including religious extremisms, are always tempted to consolidate their base by identifying a group that lies outside it. Whenever a thought system toys with the idea of *everything*, it engages a notion of purity of some kind or other. Fear of contamination becomes an obsession. People watch out for the slightest chink in the fence that marks the frontier of the group. People are anxious about being affected by impurity, that is to say, by other groups. The most traditional vehicles of otherness are called "women" or "Jews": notorious marginal agents of pollution who must be controlled at all costs. But there are other vehicles too: exiles, heretics, homosexuals . . .

The obsession with purity can get itself tangled up in the language of systems that are otherwise quite opposite to each other. Religious fundamentalism and far-right totalitarianism obviously have nothing to do with the ideals of anti-colonialist militants or of parts of the far left. You could even say they were complete opposites in myriad ways, most particularly in the latter's effort to give voice to minorities and to give a space for those the system leaves out. But they also share worrying themes that should make us particularly vigilant. Jews are today caught in the pincers of two types of speech that are in other respects mutually contradictory. On one side, the far right maintains its traditional contempt for Jews as "strangers in the nation"; on the other, the far left sees the Jews as the leading edge of international capitalism.

In 2014, demonstrators in Paris chanted "Jews get out, France doesn't belong to you!";[47] and in 2017 they were screaming "Blood and soil!", "You will not replace us!", "Jews will not replace us!" at Charlottesville.[48] Those were identical attacks on Jewish power and control that allegedly undermine white supremacy. The far right censures Jews as threats to the established order. The far left censures

47 "*Juif, casse-toi, la France n'est pas à toi*", quoted in Pierre-André Taguieff, "L'année terrible pour les Français juifs", *Le Figaro*, February 27, 2015.
48 Joe Heim, "Recounting a Day of Rage, Hate, Violence and Death", *Washington Post*, August 14, 2017.

them for being part of that order and for being in its service. There's not much to differentiate these acts of discrimination, save that on the one side Jews are made to seem less like victims, and on the other, a little more privileged. That is how traditional anti-Semitic slurs are spread—by people who don't recognise that that is what they are doing.

Here are some instances. Parts of today's extreme left-wing movements never fail to identify Jews as members of the dominant group. Why so? Why are Jews consistently portrayed as privileged people, even in a society where their safety is not assured and where, as in France, anti-Semitism kills? Why are they said to be fortunate even when their social and economic positions are precarious? Why is it permissible for ethnic minorities to demand territorial sovereignty and political or cultural autonomy—except for the Jews? Why did some American feminist groups include "Justice for Palestine" in the "beating heart of the new feminist movement"?[49] When Linda Sarsour, a celebrity among the organisers of the Women's March, stated that it was not possible to be a Zionist and a feminist at the same time,[50] she was arguing that all struggles against the alienation of women had to be "anti-Zionist";

49 https://www.womenstrikeus.org/our-platform/.
50 Collier Meyerson, "Can You Be a Zionist Feminist? Linda Sarsour Says No", *The Nation*, March 13, 2017.

that put Zionist Jewish women outside the scope of her movement.

Her answer is that all struggles go hand in hand, and that feminism must always support the oppressed. "You either stand up for the rights of all women, including Palestinians, or none. There's just no way around it." But it is simplistic of her and also disturbing to fail to name and acknowledge all the oppressions and dominations that are in play. Does her new feminism aim to reach its consensus by abandoning Jewish women exclusively, to the advantage of all other women? Why does she use the term "Zionist" to refer only to a colonialist or ultra-nationalist enterprise with which many women (including the author of this book) do not identify?

With identities and definitions reduced to caricatures and individuals replaced by the categories they represent, you get a weird mishmash in which some people are guilty for what they are and others are innocent whatever they do.

The only real way in which struggles may go hand in hand is when they join forces to protect vulnerable individuals, defend the oppressed and give to all the opportunity to assume their responsibilities—not merely as members of a clan or camp, but as subjects with the ability to cast a critical eye on their histories and traditions and to undertake political action.

Fundamentalism, nationalism, anti-colonialism . . . the risk of totalitarianism arises in more than one ideology. Everybody experiences the seductions of Wholeness— even Jews! It prompts communities to withdraw behind their own walls, or to become fiercely ultra-nationalist when they ground themselves in opposition to an Other they consider beneath contempt. It is also present in virtual form when Zionists of a particular kind declare Jewish Diasporic identity to be illegitimate or to have lost its way: for them, Israel is the "Whole" of the answer to the Jewish question, and its ultimate conclusion.

To counter this dangerous illusion, it behoves other Jews to hark back at all times to the fundamental gap that they have embodied over the centuries and which alone can function both as a barrier to totalitarianism and as a guarantee of Jewish continuity.

True Judaism is to be found neither in Israel nor in the Diaspora. This is because it is true only where it doesn't imagine it has said *everything* about itself.

The inside outside

The idea of authenticity and the dream of an "authentic self" is exploited nowadays by innumerable advertisers, politicians and community leaders. The notion that we should get rid of whatever pollutes or distorts our identity including all its oddities and impurities can be found in the arguments of campaigns and movements far removed from each other—ranging from the rhetoric of nationalism and xenophobia to alter-globalist, Zionist and pro-Palestinian propaganda. Eliminating past dominations and submissions would allow you to put history to rights and to recover or acquire your true self.

But is there any pure identity to be recovered? The French Lebanese novelist Amin Maalouf asks us, wisely, not to be so sure:

What makes me myself rather than anyone else is the very fact that I am poised between two countries, two or three languages, and several cultural traditions. It is precisely this that defines my identity. Would I be more authentic if I amputated one part of myself? . . . When one sees one's own identity as made up of a number of allegiances . . . it's no longer a question of "them" and "us": two armies in battle order preparing for the next confrontation.[51]

The definition that this Christian Arab gives of his own identity would make a perfect fit with the one that I

51 Amin Maalouf, *On Identity*, trans. Barbara Bray (London: Harvill, 2000), pp. 9, 26–7.

adopt to explain Jewish identity, that strange (imposed or chosen) historical capacity of the Jewish people to inhabit worlds and languages which in the end allow the same and the other to cohabit and to be both "us" and "them".

Would it be cultural appropriation to recognise myself in this definition and make it my own? If so, I plead guilty!

To acknowledge an inner dialogue between "us" and "them", to admit to this constitutive mixedness, is not to deny the existence of a people but, on the contrary, to assert it. We have to recognise the degree to which the experience of foreignness structures our identity in a constant to-and-fro between what is your own and what this "own" owes to others. That is how you construct your own authenticity.

I must now say something about that idea.

Sartre made it a key term in his *Anti-Semite and Jew*, where he sought to distinguish authentic from inauthentic Jews.

Sartre saw the effect that the view of others had had on the construction of Jewish identity over the ages, and that led him to define "Jew" as a creation of anti-Semitism. Put into the language of contemporary postcolonialism, Sartre denounced the colonisation of the Jewish minds by anti-Semites, the hold that "the dominant" has over its victims' mental lives.

An inauthentic Jew in Sartre's argument is one whose

Jewishness remains entangled in the image others have of him.

However, it is not clear what an authentic identity would be for minority groups such as Jews, Muslims, LGBT, and so on. Can anyone ever really be entirely pure or free of the way they are seen? Plenty of people think they are, and claim that their identity group or national status has made them more independent, prouder or less "under control". They have a point, especially for groups that have long suffered from discrimination and disrespect. However, philosopher Eva Illouz warns against treating authenticity and pride as equivalent values. Pride, a popular term in many groups nowadays, often leans towards the idea of an authentic identity that is one's own, washed clean of influences and past humiliations. The image of a waterproof self is nonetheless in many cases just the mirror image of the very same obsession with the view from outside, and partly intended to be received by the dominant from which you are allegedly liberated, and in that sense it is only one step in the development of resilience. "Pride is an important psychological resource and political strategy, but it can only be a temporary one and must not become the only flag a group brandishes to the world to mark and define itself."[52] That is because

52   Eva Illouz, "Under the Hater's Violent Gaze", *Haaretz*, April 25, 2018.

pride would then be as dependent on the other's gaze and as inauthentic as any other identity. It would be the kind of pride that says to the former coloniser: "You can see I am not what you thought I was. You can see I owe you nothing. Can't you?" That would perpetuate the dependence of identity on the mind of the other.

What, then, is authenticity, if not the acknowledgement that we do not know what grounds it? That is to say, there is in me a something that does not derive from what other people have attributed to me, a definitely-me that I cannot define.

I do not believe my own Jewishness is entirely defined by what anti-Semitism says about it. I do not believe I am Jewish only because other people have said so. But I would have a hard time saying what the authentic essence of my Jewishness consists of, or what its solid centre might be irrespective of historical particularities. That inexpressible sense is perhaps the best definition I can give. It is the authentically impossible statement of what it means to be Jewish and what it means to be one's self.

When Derrida was asked what it means to be Jewish, he said:

> Well, I know I don't know, and I suspect that people
> who think they know don't know either . . . What
> happens, what happens to me, what is the event

that takes place when responding to the label I insist on presenting myself as Jewish, on saying and telling myself "I am a Jew"—not an authentic or an inauthentic or a quasi-authentic Jew.[53]

These paradoxical motifs of being Jewish, the gift, and circumcision, are inseparable for me. In order for them to be inseparable, for them to form a chain in some way, the main thing is that it mustn't come to a halt and that you can't assign an identity, a stable self-identity, to any one of those notions. If you think you know what it is to be Jewish, what giving is, what circumcision is, you can be sure that there won't be any more of them: that there never has been any of them![54]

Now we have it. That is maybe what anti-Semitic readers have been waiting for if they have read this book down to the last page. How can we be rid of Jews? There is a solution, and it's a piece of good news. There really is a way of getting them to disappear.

53 Jacques Derrida, "Abraham, l'autre", in *Judéités: questions pour Jacques Derrida*, ed. Joseph Cohen and Raphael Zagury-Orly (Paris: Galilée, 2003), p. 38.
54 Jacques Derrida, *Questioning Judaism: Interviews by Elisabeth Weber*, trans. Rachel Bowlby (Stanford: Stanford University Press, 2004), p. 44.

All you have to do is to convince Jews they know exactly what Jewishness is. By the time you've done that, there won't be any left.

Meanwhile, anti-Semites will just have to put up with us.

DELPHINE HORVILLEUR studied at the Hebrew University of Jerusalem and worked as a journalist on French television before before moving to New York and beginning her rabbinical studies. She was ordained in 2008 and is currently one of only four female rabbis in France. She drew media attention in the wake of rising anti-Semitic attacks and vandalism in France for her consistently compelling case for laïcité and her strong feminist stance on social justice issues. She has written for the *Washington Post* and *Haaretz*, and is the author of *En tenue d'Ève: féminin, pudeur et judaïsme*, and *Comment les rabbins font des enfants*.

DAVID BELLOS is Professor of French Literature and Professor of Comparative Literature at Princeton University. He has written biographies of Georges Perec and Jacques Tati, and an introduction to translation studies, *Is That A Fish in Your Ear?* He has translated numerous authors from French, including Georges Perec, Fred Vargas and Georges Simenon, and his translation of the works of Ismail Kadare won the first Man Booker International Prize in 2005. He was made Officier in the Ordre national des Arts et des Lettres in 2015.

broadcast journalism studies in the Bishnu Lycée
School Journalism and worked as a journalist on French
television before being allowed to her work and beginning her television studies. She obtained in 2013
she is currently one of only four female editors in France.
She draw inspiration in many sketches chapters and satiric
attacks and articulation for the political and socio
political race forefront and her strong feminist stance on
social issues. Lately she has written for the Washington
Post and [...] she collaborated with Good Bye, Lenin
[...] [...] and commitment for regime? Joan accepting

DAVID BELLOS is Professor of French Literature and
Professor of Comparative Literature at Princeton University. He has written biographies of Georges Perec and
Jacques Tati, and an introduction to translation studies
in Fish in Your Ear. He has translated numerous
authors from French, including Georges Perec, Fred
Vargas and Georges Simenon. His translation of the
works of Ismail Kadare won the first ever Man Booker International Translators. He was made Officier in the Ordre
national des Arts et des Lettres in 1994.